en't

Widgets

Lucy Windsor

People Aren't Widgets : Lucy Winsdor -- 1st Ed.

ISBN 978-1-849145275

Special discounts are available on quantity purchases by corporations, associations and others.

For permission to use content and multiple order requests, contact the author at the web site below:

www.theperformance.biz

Book Layout ©2013 BookDesignTemplates.com

Cover graphic © denis_pc via Fotolia.com

Author guidance, iMindMaps and Graphics by Tom Evans
www.tomevans.co

With special thanks to my Mum, Lesley Windsor, who is gentle and kind and taught me the art of listening. To my Dad, Joe Windsor, who has been my lifelong business mentor and supporter. To my brother David, who is in my heart and thoughts every day even though he is no longer with us, and my brother Matthew, who thankfully still is.

To my husband, Michael McNulty who is my soul mate and with whom I share my heart and my professional life. To my two children, Lydia and Max who are constant rays of sunshine and providers of wisdom.

I'd also like ~~also~~ to thank Cloe Madanes and Mark and Magali Peysha who have taught me so much. Big thanks to Nick Heap for helping me find my core and to my book mentor, Tom Evans, for helping me find my voice.

Contents

Fore Words

A single molecule of water, with two hydrogen atoms and one of oxygen, does not tell the whole story of its potential. When billions and billions of molecules of H20 come together in a droplet of water, they adopt a strange quality, that of being wet.

Each individual molecule may not 'know' what they are a part of, but put enough of them together and they can create an ocean to harbour life or to be sailed across.

Reduce the temperature of water and it freezes, or heat it up and it turns to steam. An ice crystal can grow to the size of a glacier and carve valleys from solid rock. Superheated steam geysers, both on land and under the oceans, are one of the probable locations from which life came to be on our planet.

When humans start playing with ice, they can build igloos or create elegant ice sculptures. When we humans heat water up, we can make a cup of coffee or even power a steam train.

We humans are even made from around 60% of those little H20 molecules.

Those individual molecules had no idea they could make a sentient being who could work out the atomic components of the molecules that they are made from.

So, when you get a bunch of humans (or 'water carriers') working together, they can move mountains and make waves. Thousands of years ago, the great pyramids were built by a huge coordinated workforce. More recently, only 100 years ago in 1914, Model T-Fords rolled out of the Highland Park Plant at the rate of one every 93 minutes.

These days workers at Macdonald's collectively make and sell 100 burgers a second. These incredible rates of production are made possible by a workforce following rules and procedures, all matched by levels of consumption and appetite by a growing population.

Yet it is sad that polls indicate that only 13% of workers feel engaged by their jobs. Around 24% are what Gallup describe as "actively disengaged," meaning they pretty much hate their jobs. The vast majority, some 63%, state that they are "not engaged," meaning they are unhappy but not drastically so. They virtually sleepwalk through their days and put minimal energy into their work.

In short, people have become widgets. In our so-called modern society, it is easy to feel we are just cogs in the machine and individual humans, either floating, sinking or sailing, in a vast ocean of humanity.

There is hope though. During a visit to the NASA space centre in 1962, President Kennedy noticed a janitor carrying a broom. He interrupted his tour, walked over to the man and said, "Hi, I'm Jack Kennedy. What are you doing?"

"Well, Mr President," the janitor responded, "I'm helping put a man on the moon."

This book describes how a modern, forward thinking business can de-widgetise their employees while ensuring the wheels of commerce are well-oiled and run smoothly and freely. The principles explored here apply equally to large corporations and SME's. Even solopreneurs will benefit from the guidance here and find ways to free themselves from being their own employers.

People Aren't Widgets does not advocate this be achieved by creating an army of anarchistic mavericks. Rather, it addresses the malaise that creeps into a business when their employees act like individual molecules of water in a lake or a sea.

Rather than being pulled by the tide and dragged along uncontrollably by the wind, de-widgetised employees set sail and steer a course in full knowledge of where they are going and how they are going to get there. For sure, there will be captains, galley chefs and cabin boys, but each will appreciate the role of the others and as a result even aspire to rise up the career ladder.

So be prepared for a wondrous journey knowing that, when people are motivated and pull together, they can build huge pyramids and send metaphorical rockets to places beyond your wildest dreams.

Tom Evans, author of The Zone

CHAPTER 1

About This Book

Widget [noun & verb]

- a small mechanical device with limited functionality whose name is unknown or can't be recalled

- unnecessarily applying too much attention to detail

Sat Navs

Only ten years before the writing of this book, sat navs in cars were a luxury item. These days they are ubiquitous and have become widgetised. You can buy one for less than £100. Indeed many smartphones and tablet computers come with one for free.

In days gone by, cartographers were dashing explorers opening up new frontiers. These days they are mostly number crunchers tied to a computer and never seeing the light of day. The art of map reading has declined too.

I remember my first experience using a sat nav was on a family holiday in Portugal. We arrived at Faro airport and programmed our electronic companion to take us to our holiday home. It was easy! We so enjoyed the journey. It was reassuring to know that the sat nav would tell us what to do. So, we used it each time we left the house for trips out and for the return journey.

Yet, a week into our holiday and we still couldn't find our way home without it! We were dependent on our programmable friend and baffled by our inability to remember the route home. A couple of days are all that is normally needed to know our way around.

The penny dropped. We had stopped looking out for patterns and landmarks and junctions. We had effectively 'switched off', no longer seeing what was around us. No longer getting a 'feel' for our surroundings.

So, we decided to leave the sat nav behind and instead enjoyed finding our way using a paper map, road signs, landmarks and our own recollections. We made a conscious decision to get to know the area.

Free to explore at random, we found little restaurants that we hadn't seen before. We noticed the village church and discovered its curious vault, wallpapered with ancient human skulls. We found a quaint marketplace for the locals, which sold fabulous fresh fish and vegetables from local growers. We bought there rather than going to the bland and uninspired supermarket on the highway.

We felt we were at last on a real holiday connecting with the area and the people who lived there.

Sat navs are useful for one off journeys – to get from A to B, but if we want to connect with an area and with the community, we need to engage with it personally.

PEOPLE AREN'T WIDGETS

It isn't easy to just buy people in as and when we need them. Neither can we put them through a process and expect them to come out the other end perfectly manufactured and moulded to the task they're assigned to do.

The engineering task of assembling widgets to work neatly alongside other widgets, like parts inside a car engine, takes careful design and a certain amount of 'road testing'. Once assembled, the widgets are fixed in place, immoveable. Quality of mechanical engineering makes the best engines sing and run smoothly.

In the desire to emulate the efficiency of the engine, many organisations have processes, procedures and measurements in place to optimise efficiency in their people. As a result, many have found themselves facing new challenges. With a widgetised workforce, instead of liberating employees to deliver on their tasks, employees become restricted by rules and regulations, disempowered, defensive, overworked and stressed. Widgetised employees are fighting below their weight. Many miss the point of it all, and despite working hard, they fear retribution if they are seen to be lacking in some way or if they make a mistake.

The sad fact is that in too many organisations, it has become the cultural norm to put blame ahead of trust. The workforce has become controlled by frameworks and measurements, and the widgetised employee often feels devoid of any real connection. They cry out to be heard and noticed for who they are and what they have to offer.

Too often, it is only when they take days off sick or find another job that the symptoms are noticed.

Those at the top of organisations are as perplexed by the complexity of balancing operational imperatives with the needs of their people, as their employees are by the constant pressure to conform and perform. They are bombarded with tools and ideas, processes and innovations. Over time, these stack up to provide an exhausting and unwelcome distraction from the really important corporate goals. Never mind the cost and time taken to implement it all!

Sometimes the task of people management can seem like an ever moving ocean – contain it in one area, only for the water to be diverted elsewhere. Like the ocean, people are constantly changing and moving, both emotionally and physically. They have their ups and downs. Their age, relationships, family situation, finances, friendships, home, health, thoughts and past experiences, all contribute to differentiate each person from each other. They don't, and never will, fit neatly into all the different boxes that an organisation has to tick.

The business has its diversity quotas to meet, governance issues, no end of hoops to jump through for industry regulators. Not to mention the obligation to provide the outstanding office environment, subsidised canteens, in-house gymnasiums and all that is required to keep an employee happy.

You may have noticed that the focus in the preceding paragraph has been on everything other than the goals of the business – and in some respects, this is what happens when we widgetise our workforce.

People simply aren't widgets. As long as we believe that we can wield any control over our staff, what they should think and how they should behave, we are missing a huge opportunity and impacting profits.

Now, you might think it rude that I use the word widget to describe a hard working individual with a heart and soul. As I said in my opening statement, People Aren't Widgets. It is not the person that is defined by the word 'widget', but how we treat them in the work environment.

People aren't widgets, but we are all capable of widgeting and we do all like to widget purposely from time to time. When we widget, we expect someone else to make the decisions, to be responsible and tell us what to do. And we do our best to comply.

We widget, for instance, when we go on a package holiday. We arrive at the airport, suitcase in hand and look for the person holding up a board with the holiday logo on it, they tick our names off and point us in the direction of the coach that will drop us at our hotel. We have no real idea where we are going and we really don't care! All we want is a rest with some sun, sand, sea, pool, a bit of luxury, and some lively evenings. Have you ever noticed that when widgeting, people suddenly don't know how to think for themselves?

When widgeting, we find ourselves asking really basic questions like, "What time do we have to be at the restaurant tonight?" This is a question we could very easily find the answers to on our own, by looking at the opening times on the board outside the restaurant, or asking at Reception. Yet, when we are widgeting, we somehow feel that there is a right way and a wrong way. We want to fit in and do the right thing, so we don't do anything until we've run it by the tour representative.

There is NOTHING wrong with widgeting, when we actively choose to do so.

Widgeting at work is more often than not the unintentional consequence of the culture we have created, rather than a proactive choice. It is a cultural, co-dependent state. Managers take up the role of fixer and director and the widgets do their best to meet their managers' demands.

Widgetisation of the workforce is a pervasive and perhaps unintentional consequence of trying to stay competitive and profitable while operating in an uncertain, volatile economy. It has, perhaps, come about in the western world because of the trend for making it easier to reach quick decisions in order to become a more dynamic organisation.

Despite the enormous investment that has been made in recent decades on training, quality, health and safety, diversity and welfare at work, we remain as bogged down as ever by paperwork, stress, sickness tribunals and apathy in the workplace. These are the real consequences of widgetisation.

Billions are invested globally in training each year. Many organisations also have frameworks and tools, surveys and measurements that help them to create and understand the makeup of their teams, matching the right type of people with the roles to which they are best suited. There is also a whole raft of training packages geared towards improving performance.

The content of many training programmes and the measurement tools available today are of an exceptionally high standard. Yet, despite investing billions each year in learning and development, frameworks and models, values and branding, we still haven't managed to crack the perennial problem of 'people'. More specifically, the training available is only as successful as the motivation and capacity staff have to take it on board and act on it.

So, rather than keep plugging away at the 'same old, same old', searching for alternative ways to make the message stick and adding more models, measurements and frameworks into the mix, it is time to take a step back and really study what is going on.

Times are changing. Our clients are changing. The economic climate is in a state of constant change and we know we must adapt to survive. What worked pre-2007, when the banking crisis occurred, will not work today. The economy is uncertain. People are uncertain. Trust needs to be built.

Every organisation today, whether commercial or not, operates as a business, with a forensic eye trained on the Profit and Loss and Balance Sheets. Large businesses create large overheads and one thing to be sure of is that today, big is no longer beautiful when it comes to the scale of an organisation. Big has now become synonymous with inefficiency.

Organisations are focused on streamlining and optimising. Attention is being paid to culture, diversity and corporate responsibility, yet these things all have to be catered for without detriment to the bottom line.

The stress on individuals in organisations across the western world is showing. This book describes a simple approach to de-widgetisation, de-stressing and re-motivation of both employees and all grades of management right up to the boardroom.

It is a self-help manual for businesses that are suffering from dis-ease.

CHAPTER 2

Values and Widgets Don't Mix

Value [noun]

- the worth of an individual or an object or chattel

- a principle that we hold in esteem

"Strive not to be a success, but rather to be of value."

Albert Einstein

Unique Value

Laura, a successful Account Manager, shared her story with me. She worked full time for a Fortune 500 company. She was very capable at her job and was earmarked as high potential. Dealing with very senior clients, Laura was able to negotiate some exceptionally lucrative deals for her company and, as she was very conscientious, she always ensured the team had the necessary support so that they could deliver on the promises made during the bid process.

Laura was the type of employee every organisation wants. Bright, confident and a safe pair of hands that delivered, she was a contributor whose work was of a high standard.

When Laura had her second child, she took the decision to work part time in order to strike a balance between working and caring for her children. This was frustrating for the company. They highly valued her. She was one of their top performers, committed and loyal. They could see the potential she had for promotion within the organisation. Furthermore, her decision reflected badly on their statistics regarding women working in their business.

Keen to do everything they could to get her working full time, they reminded her every opportunity of what she was capable of and encouraged her to rethink her decision. They also put her on the global talent programme, demonstrating their commitment to her as an employee, that she was still developing within the organisation and that they had done everything they could to offer a career path for her.

While she loved her job, Laura felt under enormous pressure and very guilty that she wasn't able to give them enough, and she began to question whether she would ever even want the pressure of working full time and progressing up the career ladder.

Laura thought long and hard and eventually asked to be taken off the global talent programme, explaining that she had made a decision that she didn't want to take on more responsibility. The company insisted that it would not be viewed well to do so and they kept her on it.

Whenever the subject of career progression was brought up, she felt like they just weren't listening to her and they were certainly not understanding her current situation. The ongoing persistence and encouragement from the business to step up to the next level, felt to her like she would never be properly valued for the work she was already doing. Laura knew that the company had metrics to meet and she felt very much that she was just perceived as a diversity statistic. The trust broke down and Laura became disillusioned.

The company representatives were doing all they could to be seen to deliver in terms of employee expectations and to meet their obligations regarding diversity metrics. Yet, Laura felt so brow-beaten that she decided enough was enough. Far from being valued by her company, she felt unheard, a mere metric. She handed in her notice and left, and is currently working successfully as a contractor in another organisation.

Interestingly, during our conversation, Laura told me that she had been very happy working for the company until the pressure began. As a loyal employee, she had wanted to stay and would have been keen to pick up a full time career with them in the future, but the trust had gone.

THE VALUE CULTURE

Much is spoken about values in the workplace, and nowadays even in schools. When it comes to asking people about their individual values, often they haven't given it much thought. Yet, whether we have thought about it or not, we are driven by our own personal values and the rules we apply to them.

When it comes to values in business, most organisations these days have a list of values that they share with colleagues and customers. These values represent the core principles that the organisation wishes to adhere to and they are designed to form a vision, or a framework, for the way their customers can expect to be treated by them.

Defining the values and letting everyone know about them is just the beginning of the process.

The next phase is to ensure those words are put into action. Otherwise known as 'walking the talk' and this can prove to be more challenging, yet not impossible.

Let's take a typical example of a company's core values:

- We are passionate about what we do

- We have integrity

- We are accountable for our actions

- We respect our customers

- We ensure quality in all that we do

- We love to work here

When a potential customer sees these values, they get a feeling for, or a picture of, the organisation. They may feel comforted and inclined to trust the company.

Yet, over time, it is never the value statements that build and maintain the trust, but how the organisation behaves. How it relates to that customer face to face.

There are three steps towards building real trust. Without all three, the organisation will stumble. Glossy sound bites created by the Marketing team in conjunction with brand specialists, are not enough on their own, they need the support of every member of the organisation.

The three steps are as follows:

Step 1:

Ensure your Values are aligned with the mission statement

Step 2:

Live and breathe your Values

Step 3:

Align the personal values of your employees to your corporate Values

It is absolutely vital that the mission statement is supported by the values. If not, the risk is that either the mission statement is pursued at the expense of the values, or the values are pursued, which puts the business imperatives in jeopardy.

Before we can expect our followers (employees) to live our company values, we have to embody them ourselves. This means putting them at the forefront of all that we do. This requires some careful consideration.

It might be useful to exemplify what I mean by this. In order to do so, I am going to deconstruct some typical Values that are used by businesses large and small and examine what they really mean.

Imagine you are the CEO of Big Business Plc. As a leader of this organisation, in stating your company values, you have also made a personal commitment in the following ways:

- Passion

- Integrity

- Accountability

- Respect

- Quality

- Love

Passion

As the CEO of Big Business Plc, it is natural and essential you demonstrate your passion both internally and externally every day.

- Passion for the products and services you offer
- Passion for how you operate
- Passion for the people you employ at all levels
- Passion for the challenges you face
- Passion for the successes you have
- Passion for finding ways to improve

To have passion is to have enthusiasm, love, and desire for a subject, and as a leader, the best way to demonstrate living this value is to feel passionate about the good, the bad and the ugly too. For it is this passion that allows us to embrace the bad and the ugly and to create something beautiful through positive and well planned action.

Integrity

You must demonstrate that you act honestly, honourably and sincerely as far as is possible.

- Have a good moral compass

- Treat your employees, clients and suppliers fairly

- Support employees through periods of personal growth and challenge

- Act with integrity

- Be respectful and non-critical

- Separate the issue from the person and be objective

This approach, together with a strong vision for a positive outcome or objective, paves the way for mountains to be moved.

Accountability

Even if someone has made a disastrous error at work, it is your response that you will be measured by.

- Did you in any way contribute to the problem?

- How are you reacting to their behaviour?

- Are your actions honourable at all times?

- Is an apology necessary?

- Are you focused on problem resolution?

Before pointing the finger at an employee for not taking accountability, you must consistently demonstrate yourself what 'taking accountability' looks like. A blame culture and lack of trust starts with the leaders, so as CEO of Big Business Plc, you have the power to change it.

Respect

It is important to demonstrate your own respect and high regard for your employees, stakeholders, suppliers and customers at all times. This creates a model that your employees can emulate.

- Offer clear guidance

- Be open about your expectations

- Uncover the positive intent

Quality

We set our own standards and the quality of work produced by our peer group and subordinates is a good indication of our own contribution to quality. How can you offer quality to your employees?

- Provide the best tools, environment and support

- Model what quality work looks like

- Roll your sleeves up and go the extra mile

- Communicate

Love

What reasons do staff have, above and beyond the obvious pay cheque at the end of the month, for 'loving' their work?

- Give them good reason to 'love working here'

- Show your appreciation to them for investing their career in your organisation

- Ensure they are growing, learning, and recognised for their unique contribution

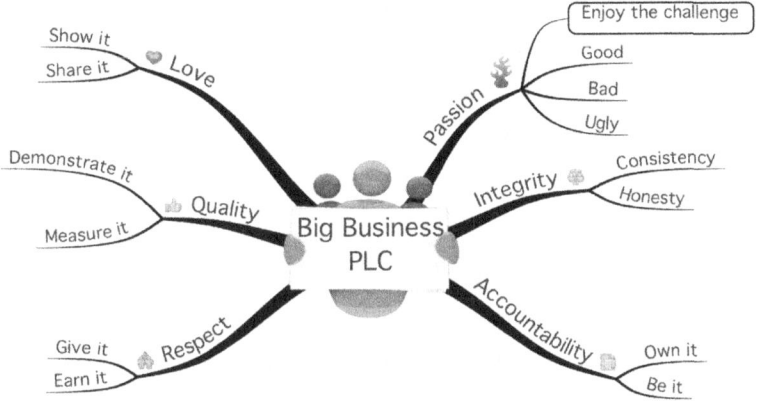

And, if you can't deliver on these promises, change the value for one that can be met truthfully.

Most people love to be in a place where they are learning and contributing in a way that makes a difference, but what that looks like depends on the person. As such, it is important to know them as individuals and to give them the support they need in order for them to 'love to work here'.

As CEO of Big Business Plc, you now have an understanding of the personal commitment behind the values that allows them to be really embodied across the organisation.

When your employees are able to align your corporate values with their personal values, they will feel at ease with them. People aren't widgets, and because of this they need the opportunity to make their own connection with the company values. Incongruence smarts like a slap in the face, so you can imagine just how important it is for employees and customers alike to feel the integrity of your values.

Our personal values run deep inside us, even when we haven't consciously decided on what our values are. They drive our behaviour, and when we feel our values have been violated in some way, it creates an intense physical and emotional reaction that runs right through our nervous system.

If you are struggling with an employee who isn't living up to your company values, who is behaving in a negative fashion, or just not very enthusiastic, then there is something adrift, which is more than likely due to a misalignment.

Either they are picking up on incongruences in the organisational culture, or they are finding it difficult to align the corporate values with their personal values in some way. By starting here, it is easy to build a common purpose and to identify the gaps.

When this happens, it is important to act quickly, before it festers and grows. Get talking. Find out where the misalignment might be, without being judgemental, and then work with them, not against them, to break through it.

By sharing, harmonising and aligning business-level and personal values, you are of course 'valuing' your employees.

CHAPTER 3

What Do We Really Need?

Need [noun]

- a requirement, duty, or obligation

- a lack of something wanted or deemed necessary

- a necessity arising from circumstances

"How wonderful it is that nobody need wait a single moment before starting to improve the world."

Anne Frank

Talk to Me!

I coached a Senior Manager, Tim, who struggled with keeping his Division on track following a series of company changes, which had culminated in a fairly radical re-organisation, including many redundancies. He felt exasperated and particularly so with one individual, Dave, a Regional Manager and one of his 12 direct reports.

He explained, "I just can't stand him. I have tried everything, but he continues to hijack every meeting with his negative comments, which, of course, everyone hears. He undermines my position and creates a really bad environment, and then the others start to agree with him, even though he created the bad atmosphere in the first place!"

"I have tried to support him and help him to understand that the company decisions were necessary for the survival of the company. I've told him on numerous occasions that as a Manager, his job is to lead his team, but he is just so negative that it is impossible to get him to see reason."

"I just don't like him. He is toxic and argumentative."

What are you picking up from the story so far? Perhaps you empathise with the Senior Manager – you know what it's like to have a battle with a 'hijacker'. Maybe you also have to manage people you don't get along with. Or, are managed by someone who you perceive dislikes you or you dislike.

So where does the real problem lie?

People may hijack situations when they feel: disempowered; out of control; insignificant; fearful or unheard. Some may not need a specific reason like the reorganisation, they may just be in the habit of being critical.

There are numerous possible reasons behind the behaviour of the hijacker in this situation, and for sure, there are alternative strategies that Dave could employ that would be more productive. However, in this situation, Tim stands a near zero chance of making any real progress as long as he is focused on trying to change Dave's behaviour. So, I explained this to Tim.

His response was one of confusion, "But I HAVE to make Dave change his behaviour, because it is affecting the whole team and they are my responsibility".

Tim was familiar with the process of how to manage difficult conversations and was growing more and more frustrated that it wasn't working in this situation.

I asked Tim, "Who was your best teacher at school?"

He told me about his science teacher who had been a great inspiration to him. I asked, what were the qualities of that teacher that inspired you?

He said, "He was so passionate about his subject, particularly physics, and he saw me for who I was. I remember struggling with Ohm's Law and he sat down with me during one lunch break and helped me to get my head round it."

Tim reflected on his situation with Dave. He realised that he too felt angry and threatened by the re-organisation, and rather than leading with passion, as his science teacher had, he had been trying to take control by telling his managers what to do without any room for discussion and collaboration.

We discussed how Tim could reconcile the change and align himself with the new organisation. Once he felt centred and positive about the future, he was able to connect openly with Dave and the rest of his management team and focus on the business again.

PURPOSE OVER PROCESS

We talk about 'needs' all the time. At work, we talk about meeting the needs of our customers and the needs of the team. Yet, do we really understand what it means?

There are so many different models and processes that we are fed in training and development programmes. These provide a useful structure or framework for a meeting, but that is all they do. It is easy to get carried away with the process and to forget about the purpose or the context of the meeting.

These models and processes are designed to create a consistent approach across the organisation. So, every member of staff who needs to, knows what a good coaching session should look like, or a good sales call, or performance review. The intention being that they will go out and model that best practice. Yet, how many employees can really take that model and make it work in the way it is intended?

There are a few who will work well to a model. By seeing the value of the model, they use it to provide them with a structure to work to.

However, when we become a widget, we hand responsibility to someone else. We get so wrapped up with the process and what we think management want from us, that we lose sight of our bigger purpose. With the best of intentions, we do our upmost to do the right thing. But, because our focus is off, the results are limited.

It is difficult to get everyone to be consistent in their communication. Whilst people are widgeting, focused on doing the right thing, following the right process, they can't be focused where it really matters.

When they are meeting the needs for the targets and key performance measurements as best they can, they lose sight of the person with whom they are communicating.

So, let's establish what people need in order to perform well:
- Do they need performance reviews?
- Do they need coaching?
- Do they need your door to be open?
- Do they need you to fix their problems?
- Do they need you to praise them?
- Do they need you to manage them?
- Do they need you to point out their errors?
- Do they need you to recommend training programmes?

The answer to all of the above is NO. Your employees don't need any of these from you. What they really need is:
- Clarity of purpose and a way forward
- Inspiration and challenge
- To know their worth
- To know they are contributing in a unique way
- To share a common purpose
- To be empowered
- To be connected
- To be learning

This is what employees really need to free them up to raise their standards. Everything else, all the models, frameworks and competencies, coaching, managing, and reviewing, are an important part of the process, yet not the goal itself.

In a decade and a half, working as a role player, I have been on the receiving end of thousands of sales calls, negotiations, coaching, performance reviews and presentations. And, in my experience, the key elements that create sustainable, successful working relationships, are being missed by probably more than 80% of the people I meet with across all sectors. They are missing the point and the consequences are significant. It is not their fault, because it seems that many organisations are currently focused on process.

Before planning your next meeting at work, list down as many things you can think of in response to these questions:

"What do I really admire or appreciate about this individual?"

"What is it about them that I dislike, or that I anticipate to be difficult?"

Next, convert all your dislikes into the appreciate column.

For example, "He is rude" might be converted into "He's straight talking and he invites me to be straight talking too."

Or, "She is defensive" might become "She values integrity. I must assure her of my good intent".

Now you are ready to plan your meeting, you are focused on the objective and no longer distracted by perceived personality clashes or power struggles. Just imagine the difference this makes to the way you approach a conversation.

The most productive conversations come from the heart, not the head, and they require us to have both courage and vulnerability in equal measure. When we value the needs of employees and colleagues, and take time to really understand what their needs are, a bidirectional trust is established where they also value the needs of the company. What goes around comes around.

CHAPTER 4

The End of the Blame Game

Blame [noun]

- to find fault with

- to pass the buck

- to shirk from our own responsibility

*"A man can fail many times, but he isn't a failure
until he begins to blame somebody else."*

John Burroughs

The Uncomfortable Truth

As a senior executive, John was doing well in the organisation where he had worked for the past eight years. The company had been privately owned, and was merged into a larger organisation. One of the Partners had left. The other was kept on for six months.

John felt his whole world was changing and he had no control over it. He felt that he had two choices. Put up, or get out. He felt angry and bitter that he had invested so much of himself into the business that he had been so proud to be a part of. So many things that made the company special in his eyes were being lost as departments were absorbed by the other company. He felt undervalued and used.

He knew that something had to change, because he was becoming irritable at work, and when he got home he would sleep most of the evening in front of the telly. Then in the early hours, he would wake up worrying about what the next day would bring and whether he still had a job to go to.

To add to his worries, he was also very concerned about his relationship with his wife. He was withdrawing from her and closing down, and this really bothered him, and he knew she was worried about him.

Yet, he felt so embroiled in the situation that he couldn't rationalise his way out of it. He realised that all his efforts so far to resist the changes, which he believed to be so detrimental, and defend the culture he knew and loved, were to no avail. No one would listen to him. He was impotent.

It was then that he realised he needed to rethink. So, early one morning, he took out a piece of paper, and on it he created a mind-map. In the centre, he put himself and his family. Leading off that, he added all the things that were important to him and to the wellbeing of his family. In block letters, he wrote LEADER and linked this to himself. As a joint contributor to the family both financially and emotionally, he realised that he hadn't been present for his wife or his children – he hadn't been leading the way – all the time he had been worrying about work.

As he continued to complete his mind-map, he began to build up a picture of what was important to his life: family, health, exercise, laughter, children's exams, holidays and charity. He wanted to contribute in a material way to a charitable cause.

With the shift of focus, he gained a new perspective and it felt exciting to him. Yes, work was very much a part of his life. Yet, it was not his life. He grew stronger and stronger with every new addition to his mind-map. He felt grateful for the eight years he had served and all that gave him both financially, and emotionally through the friendships he had built.

Yet, now he could see that there was a different vision for the business brought by the new ownership. Although different, he realised that there were many positives he hadn't seen before, when he was focused on loss and blame.

As he looked through the eyes of an empowered man, he realised that he actually had a very positive role to play as part of the new organisation.

For the first time in months, John felt his energy and lust for life returning. He made a cup of tea for his wife and himself and took it up, to share what he had discovered. At 8:50am, he was at his desk ready for work, warmly greeting his colleagues as they arrived and enjoyed seeing the atmosphere lift as a direct result of his own change of state.

NO MORE GRENADES

The uncomfortable truth is that our role is to serve the mission of the organisation. There is no other reason to be employed by an organisation if it is not to deliver on that mission. Whether the company provides products and services in order to make a profit, or provides services that are designed to enhance the wellbeing of the community and are classed as non-profit organisations, this is the reality.

Every member of the organisation owns the responsibility for the successful relationship between themselves, their suppliers, associates, colleagues and clients.

We are used to believing that the behaviours of others are to blame for how we feel. The ego conspires to create this belief. And, over the years, we have become more and more programmed to deflect, rather than accept, responsibility and face up to the truth. However, the more we bury our heads in the sand, the worse we feel.

There is nothing more liberating than to accept full responsibility, even after the rug has been pulled from under our feet, and even when we are not in control of things changing around us. As an added bonus, when we accept responsibility for our part, we find we are also empowered to do something to change things, rather than reliant upon someone else.

Have you ever had reason to blame another person? We have all, from time to time, had good reason to believe that if someone had done something differently, the outcome would have been different. Or, we believe that someone else's actions, what they have said or done, is the reason we feel bad, or sad, or angry!

Over time, this creates a 'blame culture'. A culture of habitual blaming, sometimes over small and insignificant matters, sometimes over bigger, more important events.

I call it 'the grenade approach'. We throw the grenade into someone else's bunker in the hope that when it blows, we'll be in the clear. We are all guilty of doing this to some degree. That is because when we are under threat, our ego is triggered, and our ego is geared around self-protection. It will endeavour to find ways and means to justify our actions and manipulate others into believing that we are right. It is so clever at doing this, that even we believe it! Yet, in doing so, we create division and stress – not just in others, but in ourselves too. We get angry or frustrated with the other person for making us feel bad and for making us go through the uncomfortable experience of 'the difficult conversation'.

But, blame doesn't have to exist. There are two key ways that we can develop a blame-free culture.

Firstly, we can take a systemic approach as an organisation where we need to accept that mistakes happen, and when they do, we need to be objective and address the source of the problem. Rather than chastising or criticising, or pointing out the wrong-doing, we have to identify the cause and ensure the correct processes and training measures are in place to avoid a future occurrence.

Secondly, we can look at blame at an individual level. We need to help our staff develop an alternative to blame and give them the motivation to change.

What if we took blame out of it altogether? Would we all stop caring? Perhaps this is the fear, that without someone to blame, there would be no responsibility or accountability.

Systemic Blame

In a culture of systemic blame, the default response to performance management is one of defence, projection and deflection. In other words, take cover and make sure you throw the grenade into someone else's bunker!

In some organisations today, there is a tendency for messages to cascade, a bit like a waterfall.

The Board tells the executives that there is an urgent need to cut costs, as the shareholders expect to see an upturn in the next six months. The business is to reduce costs in every area possible, and increase performance. They highlight the areas where the executives are failing to meet targets and they set financial and operational targets to be met.

The executives hold urgent meetings with their managers and tell them that they have no budget for anything other than essential activity. All activity that is non-strategic is to be stopped immediately and cuts are to be made. They highlight areas where the managers are failing to meet targets and explain that they are falling below the necessary corporate behaviours and competencies.

The managers call in their team leaders and tell them that there is no money for anything, and they are under the microscope, so they will have to identify every area of spend and request sign off by the manager for even the smallest budgetary decisions. All projects have to be reviewed for their relevance and it may be that some will be canned. They highlight the areas where the team is underperforming and remind them of the corporate behaviours that need to be met at the necessary level of competence.

The team leaders tell the rest of the staff that they need to sell more, do more, achieve more and reduce costs, because jobs are on the line and there isn't the money for additional resources.

Of course, this is an exaggeration (or maybe not, in your experience). However, I use it as an example to illustrate how a business message can create an environment of uncertainty, anxiety, confusion, self-protection and deflection.

Above all, the strategic focus gets drowned out by the overwhelming pressure of the waterfall.

This is how the systemic culture of blame is created. Shareholders and the board become the enemy. There is a perception that the cost reductions are impacting only the lower level staff, and employees feel undervalued and under threat. There is no sense of pulling together in a common direction. Communication is poor. The environment becomes one of control and restriction, and individuals put up the defence barriers and stock up on grenades.

So how can we avoid a systemic blame culture from taking hold?

Imagine the Board have met and the decision is taken to reduce costs across the organisation. There are two key questions to be asked and answered by each Board member:

Question 1: Am I in alignment?

Do I personally have the belief, courage and commitment that the decision to reduce the overheads is instrumental in delivering on our strategic vision and is in line with our organisational values?

Question 2: Does everyone have my confidence?

What do my employees, colleagues, customers and suppliers need from me to give them the courage, strength and motivation to get behind the decision with confidence?

When the Board is truly aligned, the message they convey will be forward looking; shaped by the values and culture of the organisation, and it will be one that their employees can trust. Even during the most difficult and uncertain times, employees will do all in their power to deliver, if they believe that their Board members are investing the same, or greater level of personal commitment.

But, this is not just the responsibility of the Board, or the senior management team. As each member of staff from the top of the organisation to the bottom receives the message, their priority is to ask themselves those same two questions above and to act on them.

Every member of staff, no matter what their level of responsibility, has the ability to make a positive impact in some way on key business decisions, but only if they are motivated to do so.

In many organisations, this is a complete change in mind shift. For many years, we have become accustomed to focusing on the behaviour of others, what they should be doing, rather than on ourselves, and what we can do. It will require sponsorship and commitment from the top, a framework for review and a core of cultural architects – or mentors – at all levels of the organisation, to help others to learn how it's done.

It takes time, practice, encouragement and faith.

We all crave the opportunity to be seen as trustworthy and respected, and some want to be seen as ready for promotion. We all enjoy responsibility and challenge. We love to be stretched to achieve a level of performance above our expectations of ourselves. We need challenges to stretch us, yet a safety net to catch us when we stumble. There is nothing more inspiring and fulfilling than to know we have overcome a personal challenge, no matter how small, and to be looking forward to the next one.

This is the culture we should be developing in our organisations.

Personal Blame

What do people do when they operate in a culture of blame? They seek self-preservation. Depending on the pervasiveness of the blame culture, they might do this even at the expense of the truth.

They complain to their peers about how they have been mistreated or how someone else failed to deliver. They have a selective memory for what exactly was said or done. They choose the way they tell the story so that it has maximum impact and gains maximum empathy and support.

They gather allies around them and there are always people who have a strong sense of justice who will spring to their side. At worst, they will lie. It is human nature to protect ourselves when under threat and even the most honest of us are capable of creating a rather one-sided reality when we feel that someone else holds all the power, when one side is all we can see.

We fear rejection more than anything else. This is why banishment played such a powerful role in ancient civilisation, and probably why we still have a prison system to deal with our criminals. Yet the pros and cons of this strategy are worthy of another book.

If we believe that the only way to be accepted is by being right or infallible, we will stop at nothing to defend, reject, deflect and ensure that blame lies with another. This is often not even a conscious manipulation. We genuinely believe it to be true.

Action Dictates Output

By way of example, let's assume an employee fails to deliver a report on time. The usual procedure is for a performance management meeting to take place, whereby the manager highlights the matter with the employee and agrees steps going forward. Depending on their level of skill, the manager may attempt to coach the employee so that they understand that they mustn't miss a deadline again. The success or otherwise of this approach depends on both the skill of the manager and the meaning the employee assigns to the feedback.

So, what if we instead looked inside for accountability and responsibility? So when a mistake occurs, what would happen if we measured how personally accountable we were for that mistake?

This is quite a difficult concept to grasp when we live with a media pumping into us that if we admit to our mistakes, we are weak. Where politicians gibe at and ridicule each other for sport and cheap votes.

This was highlighted in the 80's when Margaret Thatcher famously said, "You turn if you want to. The lady's not for turning".

More recently this entrenched position was brought to our attention with Nick Clegg's apology regarding tuition fees, in which he pretty much admitted that he was in a position of weakness.

The problem is epidemic. We now see blame everywhere, at work, at home and in public, exacerbated by the litigation society where blame comes loaded with £ signs.

Yet, the paradox is that when the tables turn, and we truly accept responsibility, where it is due, and we mean it, something rather extraordinary occurs. The natural tendency is for others to step forward and accept their responsibility too.

Imagine you are talking and someone talks over you. If they keep on doing it, you find yourself feeling irritable and possibly you raise your voice a little to be sure they know you are still the one doing the talking. However, if they talk over you and immediately apologise for cutting you off, you might find yourself saying, "No, honestly, I was nearly finished, please go ahead, I'm interested to hear what you have to say."

Provided they mean it, and they don't continue to interrupt you, this would be a really positive outcome for you and for the conversation. Well, the same happens when a mistake is made – if you are the first one out of the starting blocks with your head held high, once they trust that it is safe to do so, others will follow.

Let's return to example of the employee who failed to deliver a report. An enlightened manager could review their own actions and might come up with something like this:

- I didn't explain my expectations clearly
- I haven't explained the strategic direction of the business
- I didn't highlight the importance of my employee's role in delivering it

So the content of this meeting might include:
- We have a problem.
- The report that you were assigned to complete has missed the deadline
- Let's resolve the immediate problem and give the customer what they need
- I wish to apologise to you
- I was unclear about how this work fits into the overall strategy
- I'd like to explain the big picture and your role within it
- Now you fully understand the purpose, what will you do to avoid a repeat occurrence?
- What will be your plan going forward?
- What resources, if any, do you need?

Conversations where each party actively accepts their own liability and collaborates towards a resolution are more powerful and more purposeful and get to the heart of the problem. The event, or mistake has already occurred and blaming someone else doesn't make it go away.

So, instead of seeing it as a weakness, and believing we should be perfect individuals, we should be praised when we hold our head high and say, "I am genuinely sorry, I accept that I could have done differently".

This approach leads to an overall reduction in mistakes. In focusing on the real cause of the mistake, there is not the same motivation to hide the truth.

When we anticipate criticism or blame, we feel threatened. Our reactive brain kicks in and we feel compelled to defend ourselves. Any response we make is geared around self-preservation, rather than at objective problem resolution. We justify our actions. We blame the system, the technology, someone else. We will find no end of excuses. It is not that we are bad people; we are just human.

Next time something happens at work that affects you directly and you feel the urge to blame someone or something else, test out the theory.

Wait until you have calmed down and then play a private game with yourself. Imagine the problem was entirely down to your own doing. In other words, you are fully responsible for it and you are therefore the one with the power to resolve it. Make a list of as many things as possible that you did (or didn't do) to contribute to the problem, and as many ways you can think of that you could have done differently.

Leave what everyone else should have done out of the equation.

Once you have clarity, identify any changes you can make and resources you might need to avoid a future recurrence of the problem.

Now you are ready to meet with the other parties involved, and because you have done this work privately, you will find that you are less likely to feel the need to defend or deflect and therefore less inclined to pass judgement or blame onto them. Instead, you can be open and honest and collaborate on what will be the way forward. If your review uncovers a need for additional resources, make the request confidently, with clarity of thought, supported by evidence, as to why it would make for better standards and more efficient work practices.

Once you have gone through this process yourself a few times, and can see the value of it in terms of the positive response from others, you can begin to introduce it to your team as best practice.

The aim being for people to come to the table willing to be accountable. This creates a viral change that will spread across the organisation.

Another way to practise this, if you aren't ready to risk trying it out at work, is to try it at home. If you have an argument with your partner, or parent, or child, take a moment to cool off and go through the process of taking full responsibility.

For example, imagine a 14-year-old boy who fails to do his homework. His parent returns from work to find him hunched over a PlayStation and loses their temper. After which, the parent might think the situation through, taking full responsibility:

- I became angry when he didn't do his homework
- I told him he was lazy
- I was critical
- I haven't explained why homework is important to his future

- I get very grumpy when I have to bring work home
- I am not around when he comes home from school
- I have left him to his own devices

So, in this case, the conversation with the son could include:

- I am sorry for losing my temper
- I criticised you and called you lazy which was unkind and unfair
- Can we talk about the benefit to you of homework?
- No one is home after school, you need to be self-motivated
- I too resist working when I'm at home!
- Perhaps we can both agree to a new, healthy attitude to getting important things done?
- Please plan a homework schedule today and let me have a copy
- Incorporate PlayStation as recreation with time limits
- Do you need my help with this?"

When we approach a problem in this way, we tend to break down the defence barriers and the other party comes to the discussion keen to contribute positively.

So, when it comes to de-widgetising the workforce, what we must do is replace blame with new qualities.

Instead of finding fault, we can discover better ways to go about our business. This is not about going soft. In fact, the reverse is true; this approach opens the door for standards to be raised far above and beyond what is possible in a blame culture.

De-wigetising is about tackling the entirety of the problem so that it is resolved for the future and a clear way forward is established. This approach allows us to uncover cracks in our communication. We will almost certainly find that our employee needs our support, rather than our disapproval.

Tug-of-war

Our generation has unwittingly created the problem that I refer to as widgetisation, which has permeated not just the workforce, but families and society as a whole.

There are too many talk shows and parliamentary debates about what is wrong with society and what needs to be done. Too many tribunals and days lost to sickness. Too much finger pointing and blame. The wonderful truth is that it isn't down to Parliament to ring the changes, it is down to us.

We are the ones to spearhead a different culture.

Let's take a look at the dichotomy faced by organisations both large and small today:

What most employees want	What most employers want
Security	Performance
Challenge	Commitment
Appreciation	Loyalty
Financial Reward	Positivity

For too long, we have been engaging in the tug-of-war of what one wants from the other. Whilst the organisation, being bigger and stronger, is apparently the overall winner, they are often doing so by pulling their employees to their knees and dragging them, anxious, bruised and exhausted, over the line.

When employees feel widgetised and anonymous, they begin to crave personal security and recognition more and more, and when they don't receive it, or they don't perceive it, they become chronically stressed. Stress has reached epic proportions in the last decade. So much so that there is a whole industry geared around managing it.

The job for life is long gone. In fact, the one thing most employers can't guarantee is job security. In the age of hot-desking, the hot desk employee doesn't even get the security of a familiar environment from which to work. As for recognition, whilst companies have various ways of recognising good work, they often miss the point.

Measures like employee engagement surveys, as useful as they are, also represent just how anonymous the employee now feels in the eyes of the organisation.

To be recognised is to be seen, on a daily basis, as a unique, living, breathing human being. An individual, with interests, desires, hopes, dreams, fears, needs and their own personal and professional challenges to overcome.

In fact, if we could get inside the heads and hearts of our employees, we would know that they are dealing with all sorts of stuff all day every day. From relationships to finances, the expectations of family and friends, needs of children, desires to have children, disappointments, successes, hobbies, demands on their time, health issues, concern for the health of loved ones, births, deaths, house moves, affording to stay where they are. They have their challenges just the same as you and I.

Even the happiest of people have periods of extreme challenge in their lives.

Their life stories play on throughout their day, like the background music in a shopping mall, yet we expect employees to come to work and separate themselves from all that is going on in their lives. It is, I suppose, understandable. Organisations pay people to work, not to manage their private lives.

That said, we are all human beings and most of us work in order to provide for our lives, rather than living to provide for our work and some perspective needs to be drawn.

Wellbeing

The wellbeing of ourselves and our workmates is paramount, not just for our collective health, but for the healthy performance of the team.

Every person in an organisation is responsible for their own wellbeing and for the wellbeing of those they come into contact with throughout the day. Now that's something to consider!

So, if you are about to blast someone, or gossip about them, because they are in the way of you getting something done, count to ten. Put their wellbeing first and treat them with respect and understanding, whatever the situation.

If it is too late, and you have already blasted someone – apologise. It is not acceptable to blast someone at work. We know we've lost control and it leaves us feeling rather ashamed, although we barely admit it to ourselves, let alone anyone else. If we are in the habit of flying off the handle, it stacks up and causes internal stress.

One way to stop doing it, is to decide to say sorry and be specific about what we are apologising for. When we offer a heartfelt apology, we effectively take ownership of our behaviour and when we own it, we are more likely to think twice about how we behave next time. If we blame someone else for our outburst, we can't own it and therefore our behaviour is always out of our control.

CHAPTER 5

Component Failure

Failure [noun]

- to prove unsuccessful

- to miss a goal or target

- to fracture or break catastrophically

"It's fine to celebrate success but it is more important to heed the lessons of failure."

Bill Gates

Referred Pain

Katherine was a business analyst. She had to manage several projects at one time, and make recommendations regarding the IT to support the business going forward. She was under considerable pressure to manage the relationships between the IT department and the business. Yet, she was doing a great job.

She used to report in through her Manager. However, in a recent change, that layer of responsibility was removed, and instead, she found herself reporting in to the Director. She was fine with this, although she found it really hard to get time in his diary and so she felt she was rather on her own. But she enjoyed her work and didn't see reason to complain. She certainly didn't want to show any weakness. In fact, she was hoping to be promoted to the next grade, as she was handling much more complex projects and her workload had increased recently, which meant she was actually having to stay late most days in order to get through it all.

One Friday, she was called into the Director's office and she was informed that the organisation was no longer going ahead with the recommendation for a new IT platform. She had spent the best part of the year working on it, and only two months before it had passed for implementation. She felt frustrated, and tried to argue the rationale for the new system and to explain why it was urgently needed, but the decision had been made and she was told to let it go.

A week later, three of her colleagues were made redundant, and she was invited into a meeting with her Director who explained that their work would be distributed amongst the team. Already under pressure with the workload she had, Katherine explained that she had no capacity left to take on any new work. She was told that everyone was busy and it was down to her and her colleagues to find a way to share the work between them.

Even more frustrated, Katherine tried to press on, putting her recent challenges down to experience and the economy. Some weeks later, Katherine was called into a meeting with two peers to discuss a new project proposed to address the same IT issues as the canned project. She let her feelings be known and when they tried to rationalise with her, she snapped at them.

The next week, as a result of a 360 degree feedback session, Katherine was told that her two colleagues had referred to her as aggressive. Katherine was floored. She left work, took herself home and cried.

How could someone possibly accuse her of being aggressive? Their description just wasn't accurate and she couldn't bear to think that anyone could think that of her. Katherine took the rest of the week off work. When she returned, she arranged for her desk to be moved to the other side of the office, where she could ensure minimal contact with her colleagues.

FINE TUNING

From time to time, the wheels fall off the bus and the ongoing pressure takes its toll, as it does on a component in an engine. It can start in under-performance, irritability or withdrawal. Employees will take time off sick or go and find another job. In too many situations, a build-up of stress can be an underlying cause.

When one person gets stressed out and stops working, it can set off a cascade. It puts pressure on everyone else who has to take on extra workloads. Naturally, this is something we want to avoid, but stress seems to be endemic these days – both at work and in our personal lives.

How stressed do you feel right now? Are you suppressing it and coping? Have you ever thought of dealing with it at source?

Often, when we are stressed, our language gives the game away.

'Not now, I've got a deadline.'

'He/she is totally unreasonable.'

'I don't know where to start, it's all too much.'

'I'm exhausted.'

'It's awful working in these conditions with everyone interrupting me.'

These statements are typical of comments made by thousands of people across every sector every day.

What is stress and what causes it?

Stress is what we feel when we believe things are out of our control. Either we believe we are being made to do something we don't want to do, or we are fearful of the consequences of our actions, or we don't feel ready for something, or we simply think this is not how it should be.

Many of us perceive stress to be a bad thing, when actually, it is just our bodies, our physiology, making us aware that something needs our attention.

Imagine your electric wiring at home. One day, you have several appliances on the go, and suddenly they all go off. So you investigate, and you discover that the lights are functioning and the boiler is on, but for some reason the ring that all the appliances plug into keeps tripping. This tells you that there is something plugged into your electrical wiring circuit that requires your attention. So, with a bit of trial and error, you establish that each time you turn on the kettle, the circuit trips, indicating the need to repair or replace the kettle.

This is how stress works. It is your own personal, physiological trip switch. It is a useful indicator that something needs looking at.

However, modern society has developed in such a way that many of us have learnt to ignore that first physiological indicator. Sometimes we will power on through, overriding all the warning signals again and again, until they become too uncomfortable and debilitating to ignore and we have total circuit breakdown. This is when we start to need time off work.

There are other warning signs that our bodies use to get in touch with us and tell us to stop or change something. Again, many of us have developed a habit of ignoring them:

Food

We are brought up to eat everything on our plate. This overrides our body's natural FULL switch. After a while, it is as if the FULL switch has stopped functioning altogether and we no longer have the innate ability to know when we have eaten sufficient.

Alcohol

For those of us who drink alcohol, some have learnt to ignore our body saying ENOUGH, which should alert us to the fact that our cognitive function has been affected. Ignore it and over time we no longer recognise when we have had enough or able to gauge when to stop.

Sugar and Caffeine

Shops serve sweet snacks and drinks by the bucket, a huge overload to our system and so much of it is hidden in everyday products, which means that without even knowing it, we have been ignoring our body when it says. "HOLD THE SUGAR!". We instead put how we feel down to fatigue, migraine, or other ailments, and we eat something sweet to pep ourselves up.

Exercise

Our exercise switch hits us with FATIGUE. We feel tired and lethargic, yet we've ignored it so long that we mistake this for depression and head to the doctor, rather than understanding that we need to get outside and walk.

Our bodies talk to us all the time and when they do, we must listen rather than ignore them. Stress is not a bad thing. It is our body's way to bring attention to something it needs and, if we listen to our body, we have the opportunity to address it before it takes hold and becomes a state of being. Stress is like having electricity coursing through us. It needs releasing. But if we ignore it, or overrule it, the stress stacks and we become vulnerable to sickness and fatigue.

So next time you feel stressed, try embracing that feeling instead of resisting it. Gently investigate what sits behind it.

If you feel your stress is indicating a lack of control, find something within your control and focus there. If you feel unsure about the future and are anxious, focus on something you can be sure of.

If you feel you have too much to do, decide what's important, what is not so important, and what can be left or delegated – agree your priorities with your manager and focus there.

Our bodies talk to us. Fact. They always have and always will. Many of us have just forgotten the art of listening. This is the first and best step to resolving stress before it grows into something unmanageable.

Stress Busters

We have evolved into a society that is busy 24x7. If we are not at work, we are found – more often than not – with our noses buried in our smartphone or tablet or our eyes glued to a TV. For many, the screen is the first to receive our attention when we wake, and the last to have our undivided before we close our eyes at night, even when we share our bed with another.

Like hungry addicts, we justify our habit rather than admitting we no longer know how to just 'be'.

We are flooded with social networking, email and other technology vying for our attention. Many people make themselves available to their work colleagues even when on holiday. Whilst this is an admirable gesture, it comes at a cost to our health and our relationships.

Downtime, time away from the hustle and bustle of life, is not a luxury. It is necessary for good mental health.

It provides us with time to be present with our families. It is when we can reflect, take stock and recharge. It is when creativity is allowed to flow.

Time out is necessary to discharge stress. As I already mentioned, stress is like an energy in our body. It builds and builds, unless we discharge it. The quickest and best way to do this is through changing our physical and emotional state.

Meditation for fifteen minutes in the morning gives your brain a chance for stillness. If you find it difficult to switch off, because your brain always seems busy and on the go, meditation is the perfect antidote.

Walking at least thirty minutes every day gets you outside and into the fresh air. Walking in a natural space can be highly therapeutic. So, even if you make some small changes, like walking to the station instead of driving, this will make a big difference.

Exercise of any sort is great for releasing the build-up of stress and anxiety and the beauty is that there are so many different types of exercise to choose from, that there really is something for everyone.

Diet plays an important role. Be mindful of what you are consuming, particularly if you are prone to snacking. Reduce sugar and carbs as far as possible. There are healthy ways to eat that are delicious and interesting, and colourful food always makes for an appetising plateful, so it can be fun to mix lots of different vegetables for a vibrant salad.

Fun days are not a luxury – they are critical to wellbeing! Laughter is the very best medicine of all.

CHAPTER 6

Super-Widgets

Super- [prefix]

- placed above or over

- of greater size, extent, quality

- surpassing others

"The element of harmony is super important."

Pharrell Williams

PASSITIVITY

One lady I worked with, Emma, came to me because she was experiencing difficulties with a colleague she worked closely with. She told me that he was aggressive and that she hated having to work with him. This relationship was getting in the way of her work and making her really miserable as she was always on edge.

She contacted me and asked for my help, explaining that she was concerned because she felt so uncomfortable working alongside her colleague.

When we started to unravel her frustration, she said that she was a socialist at heart and very proud of her working class background. She said that her colleague was a capitalist and he took great pride in talking about his wealth, his villa on the south coast of France and how well his children were doing in their expensive private schools. Everything about him, it seemed, went against her socialist beliefs. He was also very successful, having been recently promoted, during a time when she was struggling to get the recognition she felt she deserved.

We discussed her relationships with others at work. She had a small group of friends, her peers, who she felt comfortable with. However, she felt like an imposter. She felt that she didn't fit the capitalist culture.

We talked more about those she considered to be her friends at work. What did she appreciate about them? She talked about one in particular, Jem. He was generous with his time, a real family man and always seemed to be happy. He was easy to talk to and never seemed to get involved in the politics. When I asked about the relationship between Jem and the colleague she was struggling with, she said "Jem is one of those people who can get along with anyone, he's just Jem. Everyone likes him."

So what was it that was holding Emma back? We talked, amongst other things, about power. Who holds the power in the relationships? We discussed each relationship in turn and Emma had the sudden realisation that in each, she felt the power lay with the other party. Emma was in the habit of reacting to the behaviours of others. If they were welcoming towards her, she felt safe. Otherwise, she found them to be cliquey, loud or aggressive.

Emma did not have the awareness that she could actually connect with those outside her immediate peer group by developing her own communication style and this lack of understanding was holding her back both in her professional and personal life.

We worked on developing her own sense of identity and created new strategies for Emma that empowered her to create positive relationships in all situations, not just in the company of 'safe' companions.

RIGHT PEOPLE, RIGHT PLACE, RIGHT TIME

I believe that the move towards today's dynamic organisation really began with the advent of just in time manufacturing in the 90's. This was pre-Internet, but took full advantage of the technology at that time that lead to the proliferation of PC local and wide area networks giving the ability to more efficiently manage the movement of stock.

Just in time manufacturing proved to be a far more efficient method of getting goods to market. As IT capability made it possible and more cost effective to manufacture smaller production runs, and to place and accept orders in real time. As a result, production turnaround times shrank rapidly. It was a great success. Everything from car manufacturing to PC assembly could be produced in record time, with high churn rate and minimum stockholding.

Now it is much more sensible and cost effective with today's technology to only manufacture what people are going to buy and have it on the shelves just ahead of demand.

The advent of just in time efficiency!

This brought with it a new mindset and an expectation that we can have whatever we want, when we want it. It also drove the price of goods down as new competitors quickly learned the ropes.

Almost overnight, product margins became tighter. New guys were in town and hungry for a piece of the action and, this time, they had the means to stand up against the corporate giants. Attention was turned towards the stockpile of people employed and, across all sectors, organisations began to look for ways to 'downsize' operations in order to become lean enough to respond to market forces, and at the same time, maximise the available margin.

Just In Time People

The question on every CEO's mind was, "How can we create 'just in time' people?"

Organisations have been pursuing this holy grail for a good couple of decades, and it has given birth to a whole industry dedicated to process and procedures, key performance measurements and a whole raft of testing capability. Yet, except in some stand-out organisations, 'just in time' people (the right amount of the right people in the right roles at the right time) still appears to be an elusive goal.

People aren't widgets. Whilst every company chases the dream of 'just in time' people, the efficient deployment of skilled and motivated staff is a more visceral matter. By tackling it at a task level through controls, processes and procedures alone, companies addressed only half the story. Instead of providing the intended solution, it began the process of mass widgetisation.

So, as we expand that out, what happens when a whole department becomes widgetised? Each person, widgeting away, doing the best they can working alongside each other, yet not really working together. Just getting by as best they can within the narrow scope of their responsibilities.

This group of widgets, this whole department, becomes a Super-Widget. Afraid of making a mistake, or making a decision. The Super-Widget is ruled by the processes and procedures of their organisation, both written and unwritten, above and below board. Even when the rules defy common sense and even ethics, the widgets stick to them for fear of retribution.

We find this most in organisations where litigation is a real and likely prospect when a mistake occurs.

The problem being that the Super-Widget is focused on self-preservation and protection, rather than on the organisation's strategic goals and values, and the paradox is that actually, it puts the organisation more at risk of failure and public scrutiny, rather than protecting it. When whole departments operate as Super-Widgets, the focus on a large scale is in the wrong place.

Group Culture

Every group has a culture. This culture can be as hard to understand as a foreign language to the uninitiated. It takes a while to learn and, sometimes, it can seem entirely unfathomable and not worth the effort.

The culture comes from the rules (often unspoken) that the group is operating under. These do not necessarily reflect the values of the individuals involved. In fact, they can be very much at odds with the personal values, but they are the rules that serve the group in specific circumstances.

The rules are apparent in the use of language, topics of discussion, priorities, how the group members express themselves, and their body language.

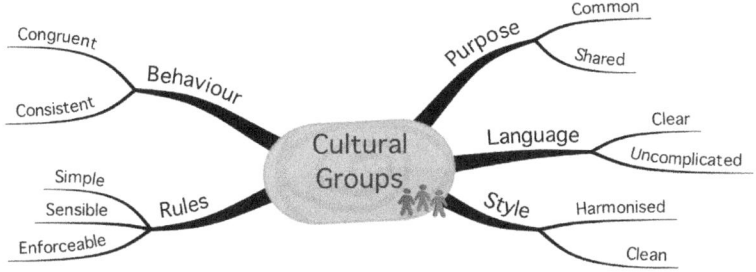

In the work environment, we might find ourselves thrust into a group and find their behaviour quite alien to us. This is because we haven't yet understood the group's culture.

In the case of the Super-Widget, for instance, where the focus is on self-preservation, the employees will follow process and procedures, and the unwritten rules and behaviours learnt from their peers, even when it is not in the best interest of the organisation or their customers.

As a new member of the group, we feel that we have two choices. Learn the rules and adapt our behaviour accordingly, or leave.

Sometimes, neither choice is appealing. If the rules grate with our values, it is difficult to adapt, yet to leave is to open up a whole new uncertainty. So, we are likely to take the line of least resistance and we adapt in order to be accepted.

Sometimes, sub-groups form within a department. When we arrive as a new member of staff, we have to quickly master which group to align ourselves with.

We assess which one best matches our own values and rules and we align ourselves there.

This is a process that is driven by feelings and emotions that come to us through our body's physiological signals (our body talking to us again), rather than a cognitive choice. This is very similar to choosing the right area or house to live in or the right school for your children. When it just feels right, we grab it with both hands.

Individuals are drawn together because they share a common set of rules and language. But what of the go-betweens? There are always go-betweens, who somehow manage to give something to each group, enough that they will be accepted by the group. They have a super-sensitivity that allows them to connect with more than one culture. This is a bit like being multi-lingual.

The Go Betweens

There are three main types of go-betweens:

Firstly, there are those who crave the acceptance of different groups – so they adapt to the different cultural dynamics in order to be accepted. These go-betweens subconsciously learn the groups' rules and languages and will provide something of themselves that benefits each group dynamic. Their motivation is personal – what's in it for me?

Secondly, there are those who seek the acceptance of different groups and do so consciously, in order to learn the culture. Their motivation is data gathering and may be to the benefit, or detriment of the group. For instance, they may be curious to understand a group's thinking so they can better market their goods. They may be gathering intelligence in order to identify those who are likely to hinder progress of the company. These type of people might be setting their sights higher up the career ladder and positioning themselves for promotion.

Thirdly, there are the leaders who are able to be accepted by other cultural groups because they consciously provide something of themselves that benefits each group. These go-betweens seek acceptance in order to influence the group dynamic. Like the data gatherers group, they may have either beneficial or detrimental motives as far as the group is concerned. Their motivation is to influence the group thinking or change the dynamics in some way.

Whatever our motive, it is impossible to transition between groups successfully, even if we want to, if we don't understand the rules and are unable to speak the language of that group. Those seeking acceptance with the purpose of 'what's in it for me' are acting subconsciously and may resent the group if they are not accepted.

In an organisation, cultural groups can either add to or hinder the efficient running of the business.

When the energy of the group is in line with the business mission and values, they can hugely benefit the business. However, in situations where the cultural group becomes a Super-Widget, the focus and energy is diverted away from the purpose of the business and instead into processes and procedures, rules, petty issues, excuses, hurt feelings, pride, and blame. This is hugely detrimental to the organisation and its customers or service users.

When group dynamics interfere with the business goal, it is important to address the problem, for all concerned. Individuals trying to function when they are in a Super-Widget environment can feel stressed, insignificant, under-valued, unloved, tired, and restless. They will be breaking their own personal values on a regular basis, just to survive, and this takes its toll over time.

The only way to affect change within a group culture is by first understanding, rather than judging or criticising, the culture and then by communicating in a language that the group can identify with.

Training, process alignment and re-structuring, are only a part of the solution.

Tribal Dynamics

People have an instinctive desire to be accepted by the 'tribe'. This coupled with other incentives towards certain behaviour, like key performance measurements, means the group culture becomes the dominant force every time. The group culture has to be positively changed to avoid things settling back into old habits.

Real and lasting change occurs when employees experience a purposeful and strategic shift of focus. To make this change, you first need to understand the culture in each department.

What is the banter? What are the typical conversations over a coffee? Is there a coherent togetherness?

There is always banter. It is the banter that we have between us that brings us together. It is through the banter, we establish our sense of belonging.

Social Cultures

In social situations, we very quickly make a decision about others. We listen to what they say, how they behave and how they dress and we decide whether that is a culture that suits us or not. If we want to be invited into a group, we very quickly learn the language of that group. We adapt so that we will be accepted. These changes are very subtle and we probably don't even notice ourselves doing it. Sometimes, we just click with a person, or a group of people. We share a language, and a similar sense of humour. It feels like coming home.

At work, we still have the same underlying stuff going on. But we don't have the luxury of walking away from those with whom the culture doesn't quite fit. This poses several risks. One is that we employ people who are like us. We allow our personal preferences to cloud our judgement regarding suitability for the role. This is well documented and many companies have developed selection strategies to minimise this risk.

Another risk is cultural. Any individual exposed to a culture over a sustained period of time, picks up the characteristics of that culture. It is not possible for them to belong without doing so. They either adapt, or they leave, such is the desire to belong. Whether the culture is one of blame or self-improvement.

Most of us really are quite chameleon like, especially those who are people-pleasers. It is not that we set out to deceive.

In order to fit in, we will say what we think another person wants to hear and this is how the cultural language develops.

Have you ever overheard a group of people talking? When they begin with a small complaint about another person, for instance, and before long they have picked them apart – their dress sense, their choice of spouse, their parenting, their housekeeping (or lack of it). The list is endless.

This is how a cultural language develops. The people talking are not bad people. They are meeting their need to fit in with the cultural norm.

So, in the work environment, we might find ourselves in a conversation where a colleague is sharing a complaint about another department or individual. In engaging in that conversation, the colleague indicates their allegiance to that culture and we will subconsciously remember that this person is someone we can bond with through sharing similar negative experiences. The opposite is also true. In many group cultures, acceptance is based on sharing positive thoughts and ideas.

In order to change a culture, we have to be aware of the existing cultural language, and facilitate the creation of a new one.

Cultural language becomes really divisive when different 'camps' begin to form. Especially when they make it clear that they are disapproving of the other. An extreme example of this arises on occasion between Board members and Unions. Where, in order to belong to one, you are culturally obliged to discredit everything the other party stands for. When, in reality, there is something to learn from all groups if only we are open to embracing it.

Training Courses

The delegates arrive for a training course, a little quiet and reserved, some even irritable that they have been sent, when they have work stacking up.

Their minds are on other things and they are uncomfortable about switching off their mobiles for the requisite period before a refreshment break. Then, there is that flurry of catch-up calls to the office, where everyone squeezes in as much as they can before turning their phone off again for the next couple of hours.

As the course progresses, the delegates begin to warm to the trainer. They get into the programme and start to share their thoughts and ideas. They become engaged in the learning. A bond develops between those in the group in this shared experience. A micro-culture has been formed.

This is a discreet, albeit temporary, cultural group. The coming together of a number of individuals where the trainer has established a unique set of ground rules that each individual accepts to ensure their survival in this group. Jokes begin to be shared. Jokes that only this specific group of people would understand. These add to the group culture and bonding.

You probably know the sort of thing I am describing.

It is the pre-framing by the trainer that initially sets the culture of the group. Everyone knows what is expected of them and what to expect from the training.

Post course – the delegates are released back into the workplace. Here, a very different culture already exists and identities have already been formed. This is where disconnect can occur.

However good the training, the unspoken and unconscious dilemma for the employee is one of belonging. To return to the workplace and to behave differently to their existing identity within an established cultural norm, is really hard to carry off.

Change of Identity

Our desire to be accepted by the group runs deep and, once we have an established identity, we have a natural tendency to fight to protect that, even if the identity we have is holding us back.

This is particularly so for 'soft skill' training. It is much easier for a person to go on a technical training course to learn a new piece of computer code, or how to operate a new piece of machinery, because to pick up a new skill is recognised as development and is not perceived to have an impact on identity.

However, to put new customer service skills, for example, into practice is much harder to do in some environments. Even when the delegate returns from the course quietly bubbling with enthusiasm, if the cultural language within the team is rigid, it doesn't take long before they slot back into their pre-determined role.

It takes a strong person to have the courage to lead a cultural change.

Individuals need permission to change and evolve and the support and encouragement to do so.

CHAPTER 7

De-Widgetisation

-isation [suffix]

- action or process

- of greater size, extent, quality

- the result of making

"The problem with widgets is that they are prone to fidget."

Anon

Wrong Directional Thinking

Tracey had a presentation coming up. She hated presenting. It scared her and she had experienced moments where she froze on stage in front of a room filled with clients. The last time she presented, she had rambled on and on and she completely lost track of what she was trying to convey.

This had been a problem for so long that she thought she'd never overcome it. In fact, each time she had to present, the problem seemed to get a little worse. She seemed to be unable to control it at all. As soon as she stood up, she could feel the terror run right through her body.

She would say to herself, "What was I thinking? Of course this was going to happen. I hate being the centre of attention!"

This was holding her back professionally, and every time she had to present, it meant weeks of anxiety preceding the event.

Tracey had a week before her presentation. It was important, to the exec committee. She was worried about what to wear and whether they would see her shaking. She was concerned that she would forget what she was saying or that her mouth would dry up. Then, if her mouth did dry, she worried that she wouldn't be able to pick up a glass of water, because she would be shaking too much. She went through every eventuality of failure, over and over in her mind. She tried to brush these thoughts away, but they kept returning. She realised it was pointless to try and pretend she was going to be able to pull it off. She had too much experience to remind her that this was just not her 'thing'.

The whole time Tracey was preparing for the presentation, her thoughts were on herself. Her failure. Her faults. Her fears. Her reluctance to even be doing this presentation. All the time she was thinking these thoughts, there was little room for her to think about the actual presentation or her audience. She procrastinated, leaving the preparation to the very last minute. Piling on even more pressure.

The morning of the presentation, her manager asked her to do a run through. Underprepared and caught by surprise, she mumbled her way through. Her points were difficult to follow and she didn't seem to really have a structure. This unsettled her further.

She called me, "Can we talk?"

"Yes, of course. How can I help?"

"I am about to present and I am terrified."

"How long have we got before the presentation?"

"Two hours."

"Great," I said cheerfully, secretly wishing she had called me a little sooner.

She explained the problem and I wrote down what she said. It was clear to me that this ship was never going to make it across the channel, as long as it remained pointed in the opposite direction.

I asked her to remember a moment in her life when she had accomplished something and felt free and excited. I asked her to describe it in detail. She described running a 10K race through the streets of London on the hottest day of the year. I asked her to tell me everything right down to feeling the sun on her back and the smell in the air.

This put her in a more positive and powerful state. Once there, I asked her about the upcoming presentation.

I said, "It's just like the race, you have a job to do. What is the job?"

She explained that her department had just delivered on a huge project, and she had been volunteered to share it with the exec committee. We returned again to the race and the friends she had been racing with. We discussed how she had encouraged them on when they needed it, and how they encouraged her when she so wanted to stop.

The team were relying on Tracey to tell their story of success well so that they could receive the recognition they deserve. It was important to all of them that the executive committee appreciated the considerable amount of work that had gone into the last six months.

Tracey said, "I'm feeling just a little bit excited now."

"How does excited differ from the feeling you had when you called me?" I asked.

"Similar. I have butterflies. But somehow it feels OK. I want to really show the execs what an amazing team we are."

Tracey did the presentation and called me excitedly afterwards and said, "I smashed it! I actually enjoyed it!"

CORE POWER

The key to de-widgetisation of the workforce lies in empowerment.

Have you ever had to manage someone and feel uncomfortable because they argue with you, or they point blank refuse to do what you say? Or, they say the right things, yet nothing changes? Maybe you have bad news to impart. Perhaps their performance is not where it should be, or they are being put at risk of redundancy. If you have ever been in this position and find it excruciatingly awkward and uncomfortable, this might be helpful to you.

Firstly, you are not alone. In fact, having met with thousands of people in my career who are faced with this sort of task, I can hand on heart say that humans, on the whole, find this interaction difficult.

My goodness, we could probably run the national grid off the energy expended in worrying about how to approach certain conversations. It takes energy thinking how best to share our message, to gain advice and to foster trust. We might get frustrated and anxious during the build up to the conversation. And then there's the task of analysing how it went, and whether our words worked and were taken in the manner they were meant, and wondering if anything is going to change.

Hours spent in stress, pain, and resentment, resulted in mixed messages, loss of trust and limited improvement. Of course, this is not the result for every difficult interaction but, in my experience, the percentage is far too high to ignore.

It is time to buck a trend. Have you ever heard the phrase self-centred? How would you react if someone referred to you as self-centred?

To me, it is the most gracious compliment I could ever be paid, yet it has such a negative connotation, that to many is repellent. Let me explain what I mean.

Self

We only have one self. Self is the person we were born with. The person that we wake up with every morning and go to sleep with every night. Self is the person through whose eyes we get to experience the world. Self knows our deepest fears and our darkest thoughts. Self is the one person who gets all our jokes and beats us up when we make mistakes.

Self is the person who is joyful and playful and loves doing everything we love to do and is also the person who gets tired and sad and disappointed and angry with us too. Self sees us naked and when we sit on the loo. Self also experiences every sexual encounter with us and every one that we imagine and never act upon. We have no secrets from Self. We are and can only ever be Self.

Centred

This means to be emotionally healthy and calm, focused, balanced. It is to have a point of reference, a foundation to return to, and inner certainty.

To be Self Centred, therefore, in the way that I see it, is an important semantic shift from the connotation of the past. Recent research allows us to understand so much more today about how the brain functions and, far from being static, we are discovering now that the brain (and how it is wired) is not finite. New experiences and the meanings we assign to our thoughts can literally change the pathways in our brains. This area of research is known as neuroplasticity.

Research shows that our view of the world is actually one that is personal to us and us alone. Our experience is never exactly the same as another person, even if we experience the same factual event, we will have interpreted the event and its meaning in a unique way, depending on how our brain is wired. We are at liberty to change our interpretation by changing our thoughts and the meanings we associate with that event.

So, Self is all we have to go by. We can only be responsible for our own thoughts, feelings and emotions. We have no control over the thoughts, feelings and emotions of anyone else. At best, we can offer up alternatives and we can lead by example. When there is a need for certainty, we can focus on becoming Self Centred, letting the drama of life, particularly the pressures of work, play out as they will, whilst being certain in our own ability to find a solution. When we are Self Centred, we have homeostasis, equilibrium, calm.

Yet, labels are not easy to overcome. I will therefore refer to being Centred, rather than Self Centred. When we are Centred, we experience a sense of oneness. Difficult conversations become something to embrace because it was the disconnect within ourselves that made the communication difficult in the first place.

Let me explain by way of an example. Imagine I am about to have a difficult conversation with an employee, Chris. Let's say Chris has been snappy with several colleagues at work. I feel uncomfortable about this conversation. I think about it. Perhaps a little too much. How best to approach it?

I don't want to upset Chris. I worry what will happen when I raise my concern. I judge Chris – "Whatever is going on at work, it wasn't me, I'd never behave like that". Actually, I really dislike Chris – Chris is to blame for my feeling uncomfortable and because a complaint has been raised with me, it's now down to me to fix it.

Have you noticed that none of these concerns are anything to do with the recipient of the conversation. The stuff churning about inside me is all about me. How I feel. How Chris' attitude is affecting me. How I have to be the one to convince Chris to change.

I approach the meeting wrestling with my own thoughts and feelings and I go in intent on fixing the problem. I follow the process of how to manage a difficult conversation, yet Chris resists with justification and indignation.

So, let's get Centred and see how it differs:

Chris is responsible for his behaviour. I am responsible for my own behaviour. I must therefore model what good looks like which requires me to understand, be open to what Chris has to say, and be honest and clear. These are the qualities I need to bring to my meeting. I also must check that Chris has been properly equipped. Does Chris know what is expected? Does Chris have the skill, tools and resources to perform as expected? Now I have all the preparation I need to come together with Chris and have the conversation.

When we are Centred, the energy in the room changes from one of separation to collaboration, and creativity flows. When problems arise, rather than complaining about all the things the other person should change or do differently, instead, the Centred person is driven with objectivity and presence of mind to reach a sustainable resolution.

This is the empowerment that most of us crave, very few have, yet is available to all.

The Keystones of Being Centred

The key to being Centred is to know yourself, know your purpose and to listen to your body.

Very few people really know who they are at their core. They know what they enjoy doing and they know what they dislike, but they don't really know who they are or the unique contribution they have to offer the World. We tend to be focused on what job we want to do.

This is the question all children are asked when they are at school. "What do you want to be when you grow up?" When a child is asked this, the grown up is expecting the child to name a profession of some sort.

It is interesting, isn't it, that the very young children when asked this question will often name a 'hero'. For instance a fireman, nurse or doctor or a super hero, like Batman or Superwoman. This is someone who they perceive to have powers that are over and above those of the rest of us.

Perhaps when we are small, we have an innate knowledge that at our core we do indeed have unique qualities that need to be expressed and channelled positively throughout our lifetime. Yet, in the society that we live in today, which is focused on material wealth as a sign of success, our ability to see the wealth in our unique gift to the world becomes tarnished.

Yet, we do all have a unique gift and it is not tied to a particular job or profession. My gift is 'Liberating Courage' and over the years I have realised that this quite literally is at the heart and core of everything I do.

So, once we have that foundation, we are already getting close to being Centred. The next thing to understand is our Purpose. As this book is about business, I will talk about the business purpose, rather than our universal purpose.

When we understand our own individual purpose, we have a direction towards which to aim. Without it, we become reactive to others and we find ourselves widgeting, feeling that others have more control over the situation than in fact they do.

When taking on any new assignment, it is crucial that we understand the purpose of that assignment and it is our responsibility to do so. What outcomes are expected? What exactly will be achieved from undertaking this task? What is expected of me?

Once we understand the purpose, we can align with it.

- Who do I need to be, to deliver on this purpose?

- Do I need to be decisive, or a team player?

- Do I need to challenge, or to support?

- How can I best channel my energies?

- How can I demonstrate to my colleagues that they can rely on me to deliver?

These questions give us the opportunity to gear up to the assignment, a bit like an athlete warming up for a race, creating both a physical and mental change of state.

The final element is to Listen to our body. If we are feeling discord internally, it will leak out of us, and whether we are with colleagues or clients, they will pick up on our incongruence. And, however hard we try, they will not be able to trust us. When we feel discord, it is the best indicator available to let us know that we have something to learn.

Empowerment

To be Centred is to be empowered. An empowered individual does not widget and does not hold resentment towards others for their achievements. Instead, they focus on staying true to themselves and what they can contribute. They are the heroes of the organisation, the pillars of strength.

As we empower our people one by one, we change the culture of the group, which in turn changes the culture of the department, and the culture of the organisation. The change spreads quickly, because as a species, we meet more of our needs in more positive ways through being Centred, than we do through widgeting.

And when we employ empowered people, we have the nearest we can get to just in time people, with less stress, more fun, more wealth and less overhead. As a result, we get a more focused and dynamic organisation.

CHAPTER 8

The Centred Business

Centred [verb]

- taking and staying in the middle ground

- being balanced and in equilibrium

"Take care of your body. It's the only place you have to live."

Jim Rohn

Energy

Robin Williams 1951-2014. This man burst into our lives as Mork, an alien sent to this planet to report back on the behaviour of its native species, humans. He continued to capture our hearts and minds all through his life as an outstanding standup comedian and fine actor.

When we talk about energy, Robin Williams is the person who springs most vividly and easily to my mind, as his public persona was alive with the most incredible and free flowing energy.

He lit up not just a room, but millions of rooms all over the world, as his antics were broadcast directly to us across the airwaves and seemed to have an unending ability to engage and delight us. Underlying it all was always a deeper message that he so wanted to share through his humour.

What wasn't there to like about Robin Williams? He was a one-man energy generator and we soaked it up.

Energy needs a circuit to keep it flowing. It needs a boost along its way, otherwise it grows weak and finally fades out altogether. The energy between human beings is no different.

We are all capable of being energy generators. We all have within us the power of positive energy that

Robin Williams had, packaged in our own unique form.

We are also capable of being energy sinks or drains. When we end up in this mode, we are the ones that ultimately lose out. We feel a lack of influence and impact. We feel others hold the power.

We can end up soaking up the energy from people around us, when we believe they have access to a greatness that fate, circumstances and Lady Luck didn't deal to us. How draining does that feel?

If there is one lesson we can take from the extraordinary life of Robin Williams, it is this. It is the responsibility of each and every one of us, not just to bathe in the positive energy of others, but to use it to inspire us to generate positive energy of our own and to introduce that energy back into the circuit.

ENERGY GENERATORS

Once you have de-widgetised your workplace, the trick is to keep it de-widgetised. The second part of this book describes a plan to create a centred business and help you manage and maintain the good practice you have fostered.

A centred business is both healthy and prosperous. It aligns neatly with customer needs and aspirations, and dovetails seamlessly with the business models of suppliers, distributors and retailers.

Once a workforce has been de-widgetised and new working practices are established, there is a risk of complacency – new workflows that create a new set of widgets, who again forget 'the why' and just implement 'the what'.

The way to avoid such regression is to focus our energies on building a culture that is centred, and we can do this through physiological awareness.

As with all aspects of life, the workplace is governed by energy.

Life is an energetic process. Everything that is living requires energy in order to survive. Without energy, there is a flat line. The main source of all life's energy is the Sun, which provides us with an ever available, free source of energy in the form of light and heat.

It is then up to the living matter, plants and animals, to convert that energy into smaller, different forms that it can process for it to maintain order at a cellular level, homeostasis, growth and reproduction. So, a plant will use the energy from the sun to create photosynthesis, which is the process the plant uses to store energy that it needs to grow and reproduce. In most cases, oxygen is released by the plant as a waste product.

This, in turn, provides energy in forms that other organisms need for their survival, in addition to light and warmth. The oxygen released, and food and habitat that the plant produces, creates an environment in which other organisms, such as insects and mammals can thrive. And these organisms too become part of the food chain.

This is the most efficient recycling system in action. Energy flowing from one species to another in consumable forms, ensures the survival of all life on Earth, unless it is disrupted for some reason.

When the energy flow is disrupted – for instance, during times of famine – it is impossible for the living organism to thrive and, in time, death occurs.

If you imagine then, that we are all connected by this transference of energy, like an electrical circuit in your house. We are constantly receiving and passing the energy along from one person to another. What happens then when there is a conflict or when one person withdraws? We have a break in the circuit.

The positive energy of success, the negative energy of conflict, the attraction of those with like minds, and the repulsion of those who stand against us. Whether we are aware of it or not, it is the energy between individuals that alerts us to the culture of any group of people.

We feel the energy physiologically, and rationalise our feelings through our thoughts.

Has someone ever said something to you, and you feel immediately uncomfortable – kind of prickly and irritable? These are healthy physical responses in action. Yet, until we are aware of this, we believe them to be unpleasant and negative, and we blame the other person for making us feel bad.

When we build a culture based on physiological awareness, we have something really special. Each individual has the freedom to find their own alignment with the organisation, and with those who work in it, based on their feeling towards it, fine-tuning until it feels right, and being alert to anything that feels out of kilter.

By way of contrast, the alternative is being told how to behave and ignoring all physical signs of stress and anxiety, until they stack up to the point of meltdown.

Have you ever heard anyone say this?

"Well I knew he/she was going to be difficult, I could just feel it the minute they walked through the door."

The reactive response when we pick up on negativity from another person is to feel threatened or uncomfortable. In this state, we often find ourselves doing one of three things: withdraw, remove ourselves either physically, or attempt to cut off emotionally from the situation, by avoiding eye contact and offering closed verbal and non-verbal responses; yield, agree and accept their opinion in order to get it over with and get out; or 'bulldoze' them in order to take control.

None of these reactions leads to a satisfactory result for either party.

This miscommunication occurs all the time, and it is because people are picking up physiologically on the energy.

When we feel discomfort, and make the automatic assumption that the negative energy is, for one reason or another, directed towards us. We make a whole raft of often incorrect or false assumptions about what the other person is thinking.

So, in one way, when a person states that they knew someone would be difficult, they are tuning to the energy emanating from the other person. Yet, because they perceive the negative energy to be a personal attack against them, they often jump to the wrong conclusion.

When we feel what some might refer to it as a negative vibe, this is our opportunity to put the detective hat on and investigate.

We can ask questions of ourselves like:

"Have I said/done something to cause the negative energy?"

"Are their other possibilities?"

We can ask the other person:

"What are you hoping to achieve from this discussion today?"

"You don't appear to be comfortable about that suggestion, can you share your thoughts with me?"

"Do you have time for this discussion right now?"

In most training, over the past two decades at least, in schools and the workplace, we have focused primarily on logic, knowledge, and on what is going on intellectually. In doing so, we have all but ignored the most powerful method of communication available to us.

By spending many hours of role play in business and being on the receiving end of thousands of face to face conversations, standing in the shoes of customers, employees, directors, I have been able to really understand first hand, the power of the physical responses.

I am convinced that the most successful communicators view a negative energy as an opportunity to really connect and explore and understand the other party.

When we learn how to harness all physical energy positively, excellence in communication is a natural byproduct. This is the way to develop the efficiency gains in people that just in time manufacturing brought us.

In tuning in to the physical energy in the room, and using it positively, we become:

Connected
Empathetic
Naturally Inquisitive
Trustworthy
Reflective
Enthusiastic
Deliberate

Every organisation is likely to have a proportion of Centred people working in it already. They are easy to spot. A Centred person is the one with energy and enthusiasm for their role. No matter what chaos or catastrophe is going on around them, they can keep their head and have faith in their ability to overcome the challenges. They know what is required of them, have high expectations of themselves, and will strive to meet them.

They are mentally fit, and aligned with the organisation's needs, and they thrive in the work environment.

We rely on those who are Centred.

A Centred person will support other employees when they need it, and will know when the business imperatives are such that they must get their head down and focus on the job in hand. A Centred person knows both their responsibility and their worth and is able to balance the two. They also know how to handle mistakes and take guidance.

We trust those who are Centred.

We put them in front of our clients and workforce when we have difficult messages to give, we ask their opinion and we know that they have our back. Centred people form the backbone of the organisation and they can be found at every level and in every department. There is no age, no gender, no culture, no religion that precludes anyone from taking responsibility for their own thoughts and actions.

In turn, Centred people get a great deal of reward and satisfaction out of their work. They tend to respond positively to situations that others might find stressful and have a healthy regard for themselves and those around them. They bring a lightness and brightness into the workplace and, wherever they work, they create a positive and productive environment. You can probably imagine the enthusiasm that is created when a group of Centred people come together.

Centred people can accept a mistake without needing to point the finger elsewhere, and they proactively want to engage with others and learn from them. In addition, they share ideas and find solutions, rather than complaining about things that don't work.

What if we could de-widgetise the workplace so that everyone could be Centred? Can you imagine how much you would gain in terms of time and resource and how much you could save financially in your own organisation? I passionately believe that The Centred Business approach will add billions to the national profit margin.

This vision is achievable, because without exception, humans crave mental and emotional strength more than anything else. Anything less brings them stress. Centred people feel self-secure, important, engaged, valued, and are independent in their learning and contributing.

CHAPTER 9

Getting Centred

Centred [noun]

- in the middle

- at rest

"Fitness, tactics, adaptability, experience and sportsmanship are all necessary for winning."

Fred Perry

Shoulder to shoulder

I used to work in an IT company called Computacenter as an account manager. The founders, Philip Hulme and Peter Ogden, were both Harvard graduates and originally from the UK.

Philip and Peter lived and breathed the culture of Computacenter and created a sense of belonging that extended to many of our customers too. We felt like we were trail blazers, and indeed we were. The culture was 'can do' and this ethos has stayed with me always.

Philip and Peter were accessible. Their very presence made me feel excited to be a part of their team. They would, from time to time, come onto the floor for informal chats. Asking questions about what was going well and what the challenges were. They wanted to know what trends we were seeing. They did this always with a smile and with genuine interest. As an employee, it means so much for the boss to value your opinion. And, as the leaders of the business, what better way to research how the business is doing than to ask those working at the sharp end.

During times of economic uncertainty, they would share the challenges ahead and let us know that success was inevitable, because they employed the best in the industry.

There's nothing like a vote of confidence, alongside a challenge, to motivate an employee.

One time, we had a backlog in our despatch department. The call went out from the top for all hands on deck, asking for volunteers to get things moving again. I volunteered, and after a full day at work I drove to the warehouse to spend the night picking and packing.

When I arrived, there was Phil, with his usual calm smile and setting the tone, wearing a Computacenter polo shirt. He worked through the night with us. Shoulder to shoulder.

Real leaders serve their employees, enabling their employees to serve their customers.

IN SERVICE

Recent surveys show that the current focus for a high percentage of organisations is on improving efficiency through better processes and reducing costs by getting more done with fewer people. Strategically, this makes sense, at least financially. However, in other ways, it can create more problems than it solves.

An organisation going through change or re-engineering is a very difficult environment for people to work in, and can be absolutely toxic when it comes to employee relationships. It doesn't matter what engagement schemes, team-building and other initiatives you have going. In this type of environment, employees are constantly looking over their shoulder, wondering whether the axe is going to fall.

The leaders and managers too, feel the discord of the situation and this impacts their ability to communicate. They get frustrated with team members who aren't performing as well as they could. They blame the team member, calling them 'difficult' or 'confrontational'.

When we have fear, we have resistance. Millions of years of evolution has not changed the fact that our brains instinctively react to anything that is perceived to be a threat. Employees working in a business focused on reducing costs and streamlining processes, know that this means cutting staff, and this puts them in a state of fear. The human brain is so deeply hard-wired, that it cannot discern between this threat and one of immediate mortal danger.

When we feel fear, we instinctively react at a physiological level as if we are under attack. This is the fight or flight system in operation. Stress hormones are released, which in situations of real danger turbo charge us to focus on one thing only – survival. In situations like the work environment, we have no physical release for our stress and the cortisol and adrenalin have nowhere to go, and thus stick around in our bodies.

This leads to a chronic build up over time and causes difficulty sleeping and concentrating. Our memory is affected, our immune system, blood pressure, cholesterol, and weight can all be affected. We become depressed or anxious and we increase our risk of heart disease, cancer, diabetes and other illnesses.

People working in a business focused on reducing costs, reducing people and redesigning processes are attempting to function effectively in what they perceive to be a hostile environment. In this state, their brains are not able to operate effectively. They will make decisions based on the goal of survival. Or, they will be unable to make decisions at all. They will find ways to 'build walls' around them, in order to protect themselves. Self-survival becomes the driving force. This is happening right now in businesses across the world, and few businesses are properly equipped to deal with it.

In the Centred organisation, all staff are encouraged to be physiologically aware and finely tuned to recognise and deal with the first physical signs of stress, so that it doesn't stack up and become unmanageable.

Being Centred also means fewer sick days, less stress and conflict, more enjoyment and more productivity, which all boils down to lower overheads.

Yet, the Centred Organisation will have to navigate its way through change from time to time. I believe there are four key steps to ensure you make the change as positive as you possibly can for your employees, before making any sort of announcement.

Step 1: Strategic Focus

If you are currently focused on reducing cost, process improvement, business re-engineering, and performance monitoring, then your employees are likely to be operating from a state of stress and threat.

This is the last thing you need when you have so many business challenges to face. To make any real change, the focus must remain on the strategic goal. Cost savings are a means to help you arrive at that goal – they are not ever the goal themselves.

Sometimes, an organisation has to make significant cost savings. Tough messages have to be shared sometimes and companies are pretty good at understanding the underlying reasons for having to reduce costs and deciding what action to take at a business level.

Some are less clear on how to deal with the personal impact across the organisation. When planning the delivery of any key message to employees, it helps to overlay the business message with your personal approach. To do this, you need identify three things:

- The vision
- Your own hopes and fears
- The qualities you possess to make it happen

To get everyone on board with concerted energy and focus, you must identify your own hopes and fears in order to realise the qualities you need to make it happen. This honesty lays the foundation for ideas to come and your creativity will flow. It's also important to address the fears of your employees head on. They need to receive enough security, reassurance in whatever form that might be, to free them up and allow them to focus where you need them and your appreciation and respect for their commitment and contribution.

These headline activities, if used in support of the commercial message, get you away from corporate speak. This provides an authentic framework that will help to craft your message so that it really connects with your employees and creates a team spirit with a shared vision.

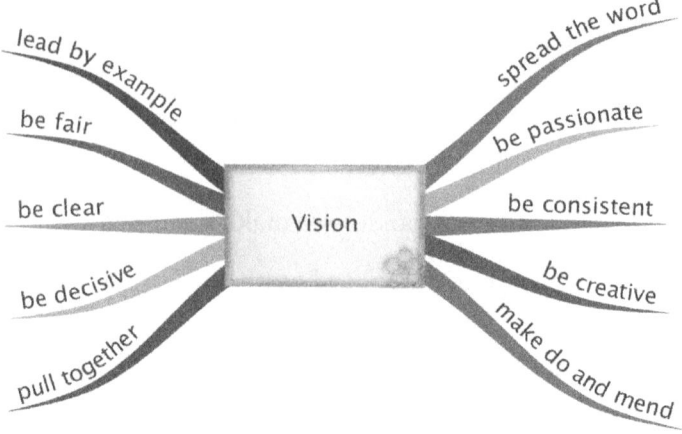

Step 2: Look In the Mirror

Metaphorically strip off and take a good look in the mirror.

- What is your organisation's current reality?
- Where are the stress fractures?
- Where is the 'relaxed muscle'?

Remember, your staff are there because you put them there. They are doing the best they can with what they know, the vision and expectations you have set for them and the knowledge, tools and resources available to them.

So, if you have some employees that are not performing, it is time to look at why. What pieces of the jigsaw are they missing that are holding them back?

Ensure you fill all the gaps and take responsibility for your end of the deal. Make changes that you need to make and share the business mission, align values, set up training and set a schedule of improvement milestones for employees to achieve. Make everyone aware of the consequences to the strategic goals of both meeting and not meeting the improvements.

Step 3: Align Values with Vision

Align your organisational values with your vision, and vice-versa.

- Are you and your leadership team living their Values at a personal level?
- Do your Values support your Vision?
- Does your Vision support your Values?
- Do your Values supply your Needs?
- Do you give proper support to staff who are struggling?

For instance, if your vision is to be aggressive in your marketplace and move to the pole position, which value would be more appropriate?

- We value personal achievement and contribution
- We offer a nurturing environment in which to work

There is no right and wrong when it comes to establishing values. It is just a matter of using the correct ones for your business and then making them meaningful. In other words, your values should reflect not just the sector you are in, but more importantly, they should reflect your culture and your culture must line up with them.

There is an expectation by staff, customers and suppliers, that the Board and leadership teams live up to organisational values at a personal level and any incongruence lights up like a Christmas tree.

Values that are not aligned to your culture, or that you are unable to meet at a personal level, will have a negative impact on your staff and customers. In fact, it is probably better not to state a value at all, than to state one that you are unable or unwilling to live up to on a consistent basis.

For example: "We aim to delight our customers."

This typical example is a value that customers LOVE, if we mean it. However, this carries with it the additional responsibility of delighting our workforce too. For, we should value them as we do our customers. Otherwise, how can we expect them to delight our customers, if they are not already coming from that place of being delighted?

It is the same for our suppliers – it will be difficult to consistently delight our customers, if we are screwing our suppliers into the ground and treating them badly. In order to 'delight our customers', we must send a message of warmth, appreciation and gratitude out to everyone we interact with.

As leaders, if we are going to make glossy statements about values, it is crucial that we embody them in everything we do. So, if you have already defined your values, and are frustrated that your staff are not living up to them, before pointing the finger of blame, take a look in the mirror and assess how well aligned personally, you and the leaders in the company really are.

Value statements are much more than words on a wall. Our ability to embody our values is what determines our culture. Otherwise, it is much like eating a packet of biscuits – nice for a short while but, ultimately, just a load of empty calories.

Step 4: Review Communication

The best communication is face to face, because your intent is absorbed primarily through non-verbal messaging and counts for up to 80% of what the recipient remembers. If your message is important, make sure it is delivered face to face, person to person, rather than relying on email. Ask yourself:

- Are you and your leadership team communicating face to face?

- Are you listening to your employees?

- Can you recognise when an employee is showing signs of stress?

There is another reason for this, and it is particularly important today. So much 'noise' is being communicated, via email, digital media and social networking. This is a major distraction for people and can be overwhelming – the noise makes it difficult to make decisions, stay focused and, over time, we become paralysed, and unable to move forward.

As a leader, take time to get around the business. Speak directly to people. Invite them to spend time with you. Sit at their desk and ask them about their day, their job and their challenges. Listen to them. Show them you are interested in them and that you appreciate them.

Share your vision directly with your staff. Be excited by it. Let your employees know that you want them to share in and be a part of the future success of your organisation.

Be honest. Be open. Be clear.

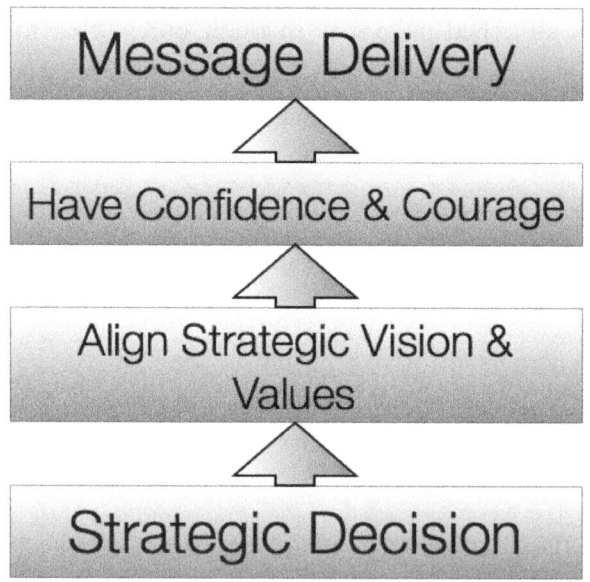

People pull out all the stops for great leaders because they believe that they can make a difference, and they believe their efforts will be appreciated.

So, if you are a leader, set your expectations and ensure your staff are adequately skilled for the job. If not, accept full responsibility for the capability gap. You, or someone in your organisation, took the decision to put them in the role they are in. If they are not performing to the level they need to be, that is your problem as much as it is theirs.

They are doing the best they can with what they know, and the resources they have available to them, and they deserve the opportunity to improve.

Be absolutely clear. Create a vision for your employees. Identify where they are today, and build a clear plan together with them, which includes appropriate objectives and milestones that they can achieve.

There are processes and tools galore on the market to facilitate increased performance, yet all too often, a performance review meeting is seen as the process. The manager may merely identify the strengths and weaknesses and then makes steps to fix the issues. And, just like a widget being manufactured on the production line, the employee feels anonymous.

Performance excellence is not determined by process. It is determined by face to face communication, by listening, by being present, by feeling the energy and directing it effectively.

Process is important. It is like the road on which a car will travel. It smooths the way. However, the driver is focused not on the road surface itself, but on his or her destination and the reason they have for making the journey.

It is important therefore, to focus not on the process, but on your purpose.

There are no shortcuts. Shortcuts just make things harder in the long-run and they don't improve performance.

In short, the most direct route to performance improvement is as follows:

- Be congruent with your values
- Stay focused on your company strategy
- Accept today's reality whilst designing tomorrow's
- Set challenging objectives with milestones
- Be in touch with your staff
- Let them know how lucky you are to have them on your team
- Be the leader you want your staff to be

I believe we are all leaders. It doesn't matter where you are in the organisation, who you are, your background or the size of the circle of influence you have. Apply these principles and you will have a fulfilling and successful career.

CHAPTER 10

Impact from the Centre Out

Impact [noun or verb]

- when two or more bodies connect

- the force with which collision is created

- leaving a memory behind of our presence

"A life is not important except in the impact it has on other lives."

Jackie Robinson

It's ALL about me

Mark worked for a tech company. He worked exceptionally hard and very long hours. He provided the safe hands to run the most challenging projects. As a conscientious type, Mark wanted recognition for the quality of his work. He did not blow his own trumpet or play politics in order to make progress in his career. He felt uncomfortable around those who did, because he felt they lacked integrity.

Yet, ten years on and Mark had reached a glass ceiling. No matter how hard he worked, or how many successful projects he delivered, he wasn't getting the recognition he deserved or wanted.

Mark decided to work through what was going on. He wrote down what he believed to be his role: "I am the one who gets lumbered with the hardest projects, because no one else can do them".

Next, he wrote down all that he did over and above the call of duty. It was a long list.

Finally, he wrote down how he felt: "Invisible; undervalued; frustrated; tired; resigned; trapped."

He looked at that piece of paper for a couple of days: at breakfast; on the train; when he went to bed. Just looked. Not an inspiring read.

On the third day, whilst in the shower, a thought struck him and he felt a surge of excitement.

He took another piece of paper and wrote: "I achieve the unachievable".

And from that place of self-assurance, he wrote all the positive attributes he brings to his role:

"Strength; focus; power; wisdom; passion; hope; commitment; vision; connection; humour; confidence."

He had unblocked the flow of energy inside him and felt a great sense of freedom.

He decided from that moment, "It is ALL about me. He kissed his wife and set off for work light of heart and glowing like the kid from the Ready Brek ad."

THE STATUS DILEMMA

I was first introduced to the idea of human needs psychology by my husband. Mike shared that his late Father, John McNulty, used to explain situations and decisions to him in terms of Maslow's theory of human needs, from time to time as he grew up. John had made human needs a way of life for him and his family, using it to make key decisions about how to support his wife and children as they grew and met challenges of their own.

In my growing up years, I had been brought up to believe two things: "Put the needs of others before your own". This was Mum's mantra, which served me pretty well in many ways, and tripped me up at times too. And, "There is no such thing as an unselfish act".

If taken at face value, the two may seem contradictory, but this is not the case. If you put the needs of others before your own, you are getting benefit from that – the feel good factor of being gracious, the giver, the provider, the fixer, the solver. So it is not an unselfish act. I knew these two things to be true (at least to me). Yet, they got me into several scrapes at work and socially.

I wanted to make sense of the two beliefs that were dominating my thoughts.

- Maslow's theory and putting the needs of others before my own

  - There's no such thing as an unselfish act

Maslow's theory was first introduced in 1943 in a paper titled "A Theory of Human Motivation". He developed a five stage model that described human behaviour and he concluded that humans have to meet each stage in the hierarchy, and we must achieve each in order.

Maslow's Five Stages

Biological and Physiological

These are the primal needs that every human being has. The need to breathe air, eat, drink, have shelter and warmth, to procreate, and to sleep.

Security

Just above primal needs are being safe from the elements, to have order and structure, boundaries, stability, and to be free from fear.

Social

Once our primal needs and safety are addressed, we have a desire for belonging, achieving, to receive love and connection, and sex.

Self Esteem

As an individual, we feel the need to have respect, status, and recognition.

Self-actualisation

As an individual operating in more complex society, we imbue ourselves with morality, creativity, prejudiced, problem solving, acceptance, and spontaneity.

Conflicting Beliefs

During my research, I came across the more current work of Tony Robbins and Cloe Madanes. Tony Robbins has redefined Maslow's Theory to make it more accessible and he has partnered up with Cloe Madanes to bring a deeper understanding to human behaviour. To my mind, the work of Robbins and Madanes is probably the most powerful and relevant work being done right now in promoting greater harmony and effectiveness in communication in a commercial, personal and social context.

We have evolved and we are no longer living in caves, hunting and being hunted, yet our needs are as relevant today as they have ever been. We have become adept at finding different ways of meeting our needs within the environment we are in, based on our experience and the meaning we assign to it. So, no matter how many billion years' of evolution, we are as governed by our compulsion to have our needs met now as we have ever been.

So, how do I reconcile that against putting the needs of others before my own? It goes back to my initial conundrum. On the one hand, I believe I am focused on the needs of others, and therefore, not my own needs. On the other hand, this is a psychological impossibility. Today, our lack of understanding of this, screws up the opportunity for successful relationships.

When we are 'putting the needs of others before our own', unless we understand what their needs are, we are likely to have a rather literal interpretation.

The Wrong Track

For instance, when a toddler wants a toy that is upstairs in his bedroom, we might see him struggling to climb the stairs, saying 'train' as he conquers each step. So we realize that he wants the train and mindful of the dangers of climbing, we scoop the boy up in our arms and run up and get the toy for him.

We are then surprised when the ungrateful boy throws the train on the floor and bursts in to angry tears. Yet he wasn't being ungrateful at all. We had just misinterpreted his need. What he really needs is to learn to climb and test his limits of physical dexterity. The anticipation of the toy in the bedroom merely supplies him with the motivation to do so.

We can meet his need, and keep him safe, by following along behind, ready to catch him if he falls. It is merely a matter of risk assessment.

Our role in this example therefore is to encourage and support him as he climbs all the way to the top so that he can have the feeling of accomplishment and develop trust in himself and his capability.

In the workplace, we think that people need our expert opinion, this model, or this version. We push things at people, giving them the solution.

We do this because we want to serve them and we seek approval. We anticipate a positive response to our efforts.

"Look at me, see how much I know! See what I have done for you."

However, if the other person's need does not match with what we have offered, they are likely not to accept our opinion or idea.

When we misjudge the need, despite all our best intentions, we are unlikely to receive the appreciation and applause we were anticipating, and then we feel crushed and we blame them.

The paradox is that those who believe they are the most giving and unselfish are those who endeavour to put the needs of others before their own. Just like the parent in my story, they can come across to the receiver as the game spoiler, self-serving or untrustworthy.

Conversely, those who put their own needs first, who don't really consider the needs of others at all, can come across as charismatic and generous. They might appear to go out of their way to please but, behind the scenes, they are merely manipulating the situation in order to get something they want. This is the other extreme.

There is no such thing as an unselfish act. Everything we do is designed to serve our own human needs. When we understand the relationship between Maslow's theory, putting the needs of others before our own, we are well on our way to cracking the perennial problem of people.

Matching Needs

Let's look at an example. A sales person, Dan, works in a garage selling cars and in walks a potential customer, Sally. The sales person needs to make as many sales as possible and is therefore keen to influence Sally into buying one of the cars in the showroom.

Dan is therefore engaging in a selfish act. He is there to sell cars in order to make commission and as a result, earn an income to create the lifestyle he wants for himself and his family.

He is also meeting his own needs. He is meeting his need for security because he knows that the action of selling cars will allow him to provide for his family; and self-esteem because for each car he sells, he will feel a personal boost. If he manages to sell more cars than his colleagues over the month, he will receive the accolade of 'top salesperson' – and will effectively be 'king of the jungle'.

Dan however, doesn't like to think of himself as self-serving. He would say that he puts the needs of the customer first. He asks Sally questions about the car she wants to buy. He will ask her, how many miles will she be driving each year. Does she want the model with the sunroof? Which wheels does she like best? He will explain the features available on the car that Sally is drawn towards. He will show her the size of the boot, and put the radio on for her to hear. Sally's eyes light up when she sees the model with the soft top and Dan agrees that she would enjoy driving this one.

Dan really believes that he puts Sally's needs before his own. He justifies this to himself because he would never try to up-sell her into a car that she hadn't expressed an interest in, or sell additional items that she doesn't need.

However, if you look at the story so far, the customer comes third on the list after his financial security and self-esteem. There is no such thing as an unselfish act, and our needs are met by our actions. Dan struggles with selling cars. He only feels comfortable with certain customers. He avoids 'difficult' or 'disrespectful' customers and find it difficult to sell at premium price, because he doesn't like to be seen as lacking integrity.

Let me introduce you to Dan's colleague, Simon. He is comfortable with the fact that he is there to make money. Simon is absolutely justified in making as much margin as possible and assumes therefore that the customer understands this. His family rely on him, after all and he is not going to accept being anything less than top of the league table each month.

He accepts too that everything he does meets his own needs. He is driven by the need for security and importance. Selling cars means he can have the holidays he wants and he feels good that others can see how successful he is.

Finally, he recognises that the customer is just like him – there to meet their own needs, through the purchase of a car. So all he has to do is find out what their needs are and he knows he can give them everything they want. So, that is the quest he sets for himself. He wants to know, is Sally worried about security and safety?

Does she like to be in control of things? Does she want to be perceived as serious or fun loving?

Sally explains to Simon that she wants the car because she needs to be in control of her finances. She hates surprises. It must therefore be reliable (she uses it to get to work) and cheap to run. When her daughter turns 17 in a few months' time, she will be learning to drive in it, so she wants to keep the insurance as low as possible.

She is drawn towards the soft top car and her eyes light up. Simon explains that she will not be able to get insurance for her daughter on that car until she is 21 and has held a full driving license for 12 months.

He directs her instead towards an alternative model that will be accepted by the insurers, has a low capacity engine, so will keep the insurance costs as low as possible, but still has some 'fun' features.

The car is merely a catalyst for Sally to meet her needs. It is not the need itself and once Simon has Sally's story, he is able to replay it to her, integrating the best model to suit all her needs and completing her vision. Simon sells the car at a premium price and Sally is happy.

A Centred organisation enables people to understand each other in order to build powerful relationships. In the centred organisation, everyone is a leader. We can all become Centred and create outstanding relationships, both at work and at home, to elevate ourselves out of the drudgery of widgeting, and to connect with others better.

Centred people put the relationship at the core of everything they do. Because they are in charge of their own emotions, they are open to understanding the emotions of others, creating mutual respect and confidence. They are genuine givers, yet they are honest enough to know that they are meeting their own needs too. They are committed and inspiring. They are here to serve and they also know when to accept the service of others.

CHAPTER 11

Sustain the Centre

Sustain [verb]

- to maintain something at a certain level

- to continue for a length of time

- to exist harmoniously and ecologically with the external environment

"Only he is successful in his business who makes that pursuit which affords him the highest pleasure sustain him."

Henry David Thoreau

The Man

I had written another piece intended for insertion here. However, thanks to the wonders of social media, something caught my eye and I made a last minute change. I felt compelled to incorporate this story because to me it demonstrates the pure, positive power of being centred.

Trending across the Internet recently was a video made at Net-a-Porter. Mark Sebba, the Chief Executive for eleven years, was due to step down on 31st July 2014. As he arrived at work one morning, he was greeted by his entire office, who had planned a moving and heartfelt tribute to their boss.

What was about to unfold was introduced by a Gospel singer, who said, "Mark, welcome to the office. This is your world."

And he led Mark through the offices while singing, with the support of a full gospel choir, "You can tell everybody … he's the man, he's the man, he's the man."

Mark put his bag down and scratched his head, and followed, taking it all in. As his delighted employees watched him pass, they danced and held up pictures of him and posters with "Mark Sebba. You be the Man" written on them.

Dancers and acrobats pranced and cartwheeled across his path as he took the long walk through the office.

At one point, he stopped in front of a video screen, where employees based in Manhattan, New Jersey, Hong Kong, Shanghai and Charlton all joined in the love fest.

"It's time to say job well done. You're the boss, you're the greatest one." The singer called him on and, as they passed four men wearing Mexican sombreros and strumming guitars, he sang, "He has all the answers to our questions" and "He's a good thing between yin and yang, he brought profits to the fashion game. He's a soldier, standing on his feet, no surrender and no retreat."

Despite this unexpected and overwhelming tribute, Mark Sebba kept his composure and it was clear to me, watching it, that his focus throughout was on allowing his team to enjoy their moment, as he made an attempt to connect personally with as many people as he could.

As he continued his walk, two dancers wearing extravagant head dresses, and even a Scottish piper, in full attire, encouraged him along.

Finally, Mark Sebba arrived at his desk, to be passed his cup of coffee. He stood and applauded his employees. He was given a microphone into which he said, "Thank you very much, everybody. I'm a bit overwhelmed. How about getting back to work?"

Just another ordinary day at the office.

So moved by this video, I contacted Mark Sebba to ask him for an interview. To be honest, I wasn't expecting a reply.

I awoke the next morning to see a message from him – he had responded promptly, so I wasn't left wondering.

Firstly, he thanked me for contacting him, acknowledging my request.

Next, he very graciously declined the interview. This was a glimpse of the 'soldier'. Clear and resolute.

Then, he explained that he was flattered to have been asked, demonstrating a humility that is rare in the work environment today.

Finally, he wished me luck with my book, parting on good terms and a positive note.

So, in my brief correspondence with Mark Sebba, after my unsolicited approach to him, I experienced his integrity, humility and decisive nature first hand and already have a good idea as to how he has managed to touch the hearts of his employees.

Natalie Massenet, founder of Net-a-Porter said, "Since 2000, Net-A-Porter has championed innovation, creativity, technology and customer service and, at its heart, has been a man of incredible integrity, wisdom and strength. Not only has he grown our business exponentially and healthily, and guided us through our sale to Richemont – he has also brought calm and confidence to the core of our group."

We can all be our own version of "The Man" and we don't need to be Chief Executive, or indeed, a man, to do so. Wouldn't work be a much better place if more of us took a leaf out of Mark Sebba's book?

THE FIVE S's

We have to stop producing widgets in the workplace. People will always be people. We are human, and sometimes things won't go as well as we would hope and mistakes will be made. Things will be said that will be regretted, and feelings will get the better of us, but when we care enough to help our people to become Centred, we allow space for better conversations to take place.

We really do have the power to reduce some of the billions spent on trying to force people to conform without understanding properly what motivates them to excel.

The five S's of the Centred employee:

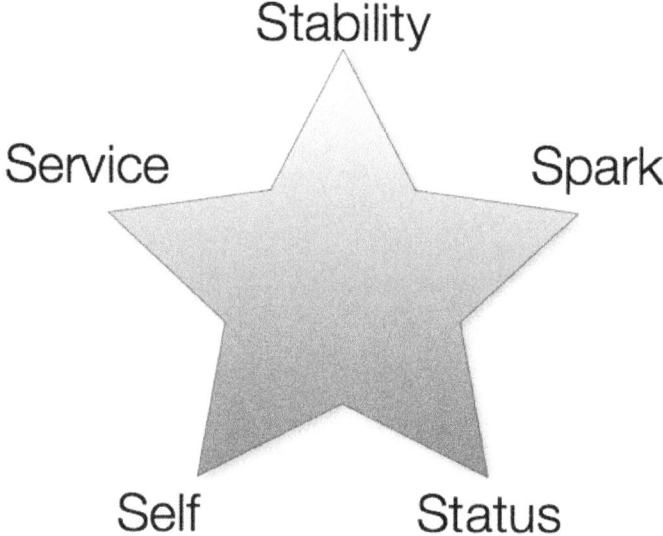

Stability

Centred employees have inbuilt stability. They know in their heart that they are doing the best they can with what they know and the tools and resources available to them. If their knowledge, tools and resources are inadequate in any way, they know how to recognise the deficiency and propose a solution, or to ask for help. They consistently demonstrate through their behaviour that they have integrity and can be trusted.

Spark

They recognise that when something goes wrong or doesn't go to plan, this is merely an opportunity to spark their creativity and problem solving and to connect, rather than withdraw. Ultimately, it is an opportunity to grow.

Status

They see every role as important and whether they are the cleaner, or the CEO, they focus on making the most of their role and how best to be of service for the greater good of the whole.

Self

They focus on their own personal evolution. Every problem becomes an opportunity to meet and overcome, rather than something to fear. Confrontations or misunderstandings become an opportunity for self-discovery and collaboration, rather than a reason to blame.

Service

Employees who are in service are both curious and interested. They look for opportunities to serve others and to introduce appropriate support where necessary. They get great personal satisfaction from making a positive contribution, no matter how small, to their colleagues, customers and stakeholders.

CHAPTER 12

After Words: Finding the Fun

Fun [noun]

- something that provides amusement

- an enjoyable endeavour

- something that makes us laugh

"Just play. Have fun. Enjoy the game."

Michael Jordan

LIGHT TOUCH WITH HIGH EXPECTATIONS

Playfulness results from being Centred.

A lightness of heart, the delight of a new connection, a togetherness of spirit even during a difficult conversation, and the thrill of shared ideas.

If you recollect your childhood and think of events where you were playful, you might think back to a time shared with another, either people or pets – your creativity flowing, laughing, open, together; maybe exploring, climbing, or making something. Or, maybe you were on your own, developing a story or ideas, making something, engrossed in a project, dancing or making up an adventure where you play the hero. You are likely to feel connected with your Self and feel Centred – invincible.

This playfulness and lightness of attitude opens up the doors of creativity and lends itself to positive outcomes, and a can-do approach.

Just like football, or basketball or any other sport, life plays out and work is a part of that. We have challenges, we have highs and we have lows. Sometimes we feel we are winning. Sometimes, we feel that we can't do right. But, even during the times when our confidence is dented, and we have had a series of knocks, even when we are at our lowest ebb, we can choose how we respond. When we practice being Centred, we can create something positive during even the toughest of times.

Can you remember striving for something, be it at work or at home, but for some reason, it seems like an immense personal challenge? It could be a presentation you gave, or a promotion you yearned for. Perhaps it was finding the resources to be the caregiver to someone who was poorly. Yet, it seems that the mountain you are climbing keeps releasing boulders that come bouncing down the slopes towards you.

When this happens, we know about it. We feel the discomfort of it in our body. It feels like a build-up of intense energy that we need to discharge. Depending on what meaning we associate with that feeling, we will describe it differently.

We might say we feel heavy, anxious, scared, angry, frozen, or nauseous. Equally, we might say we feel excited, pumped, fired up, exhilarated, or focused. However we describe it, until it is discharged, we feel it intensely throughout our whole nervous system.

If we associate a negative emotion to the feeling, we are going to find it difficult to discharge the energy building up inside us. We are likely to close down, retreat, and cut off, and we find ways to protect ourselves.

Yet, the energy has to come out somehow, so we might do anything we can to escape that feeling, and release it through anger, or go for a drink, have a smoke, eat, or take a tablet and sleep. Anything that takes away the uncomfortable feeling coursing through our body.

However, when we assign a positive emotion to the feeling, we feel this discord as a cue to take action.

It is said that just before Bruce Springsteen goes on stage, when he hears the crowd cheering, he gets an intense feeling right through his body. A surge that affects his entire nervous system and makes his heart pump faster and his palms sweat. He explains this as an important part of his preparation. Without it, he wouldn't be able to perform with the power and passion that he does. He recognises this as positive energy and channels it.

On the other hand, there are other performers, who describe the exact same experience and they call it stage fright. Some become so debilitated that they pull out of public performing altogether.

The same symptoms, with different interpretations render us either powerful or paralysed.

Listen to your body and read the signals it offers you positively. Feel the intensity of it. Assume the feeling is there for you, to guide you, to raise your game, rather than working against you. Interpret the signals your body sends you in a way that empowers, rather than hinders you. Feel the sensations as they take over your nervous system and find a positive interpretation, just as Bruce Springsteen does.

This ability to proactively respond to the signals our bodies give us is, in my opinion, one of the prime differentiators between the most successful and the average performers.

This is empowerment, and with empowerment comes freedom.

So, let's get back to playfulness. What are the rights and wrongs of treating life and work like a game? Well, again, it depends on your interpretation.

What does this sentence mean to you?

Life is a game.

- Does it inspire you to want to win?
- Is it a clarion call to have fun?
- Does it ask you to raise your game?

If life is a game, every opportunity calls us to raise our standards. If something isn't working out how we want it to, then we have a choice. We can change our expectations, or raise our game. This might mean a slight change in tactics, learning something new, or taking on fresh ideas from someone who has a different approach. We always have that choice, no matter what challenge we are faced with.

Raising the Bar

When we see life and work as a game, we are free to just change it up when things get tough. Let's face it: we all have times of real challenge. Sometimes so serious, that there is life on the line. Of course, we could set about acknowledging the gravity of the situation and focusing our efforts there, on consoling ourselves and others at the terrible fate that has befallen us. Or, we can use it as an opportunity to raise our standards and to become stronger through it.

Often we aren't the solution and we certainly aren't the problem, but somewhere along the line, we can be present. We can connect, rather than avoid. We can accept, rather than pretend. We can be calm even when all else is out of control. Our Self is the only person we have any control over and how we respond is our choice. In this way, life is a game. When all appears to be against us, we can keep playing, change our strategy, change our tactics, and up our standards.

At work, there are times of unbelievable challenge. Yet, our destiny is always within our control. That is the game. If things aren't working out in the way we want, we have the choice to change our perspective, or to up our performance. We can raise the bar in terms of our standards. We can completely change our approach if the method we are using isn't delivering the results we want or need.

We can ask for help from someone who would have a different tactic.

We all view life through our own experience. Whether we want to believe it or not. Everything we do stems from our unique perspective. The decisions we make are based on the knowledge we have and our belief system.

The meanings we associate with our feelings are based on our own habit, and we have the freedom to choose different meanings, if our existing meaning isn't giving us the results we want.

Therefore, if everything in life is about what we feel, think and do, and not about what others do, what possible reason could there be not to find the playfulness in life and work and take every single opportunity to up our standards and make the most of the game?

This book is intended to spark debate and inspiration. It is high time we elevated ourselves and took a strategic look at how we can better channel the resources and talents of the people who work in our businesses and organisations.

Values and company identity only ring true when there is a strong cultural base underneath, supporting them.

Values are important to an organisation, and they need to reflect and support the true mission of the business.

Corporate values must be lived by the leaders in the business, not just at a corporate level, but at a personal level too. That is the way to inspire employees, and to wow customers.

People aren't widgets. We have to give them what they need in order for them to perform at a high level of excellence. This means helping them to align themselves with the corporate values and to live up to them the way that is meaningful to them.

The grenade approach doesn't work. It never has done and never will. If we want our employees to take responsibility, we have to take responsibility ourselves and demonstrate what good looks like. Make blame redundant.

Stress is the accumulated effect of widgetisation. Focusing tactically, and overriding the physiological indicators that something needs attention will eventually lead to component failure.

In order for progress to be made and to be sustainable, we need to recognise that cultural language exists and is at the heart of peer pressure. In order to change or have any influence at all over cultural language, we must first learn to understand it for what it is, without judgement.

Centred people are the backbone of the Centred organisation. This is a strategic approach that keeps you and your employees focused on your business imperatives, and at the same time, allows for diversity, creativity and flow, and reduces stress and operational overheads.

There is not one person in the whole of humanity who doesn't crave to be heard. We each have our perspective on life that is constructed as a result of a lifetime of experiences as unique as our fingerprint. Each one of us has something special to give and we are delighted when we are able to do so.

Nothing crushes a person more than to feel they haven't contributed, or that their contribution was of little value, or was not good enough.

We are all doing the best we can with the tools and knowledge that we have today. Tomorrow we will know more and have more tools and resources available to us. Whatever rung of the corporate ladder we are on, we are all learning. As we develop a Centred organisation, we open the doors for learning to take place and the cultural language to be one of can-do, rather than one of blame.

I wish you luck, love and future success.

ABOUT THE AUTHOR

Lucy Windsor specialises in face to face communication. Her passion is helping people improve communicate not only at work, but at home too.

In studying human behaviour in the capacity of a business role player, Lucy became fascinated by the different ways people would approach the same exercise, when all other factors remained exactly the same.

Spurred on, Lucy began to study with the aim of identifying which secret ingredients lie behind successful communication.

She discovered that introversion and extroversion do not seem to play any significant role. And whilst process and structure does feature in most successful communication transactions, it is also true to say that they are not the determining factors. Some individuals follow the process and structure of a meeting very well, but do not manage to engage the other party.

This book identifies the key ingredients that lend themselves to productive, positive communication and it is Lucy's aim that it becomes a useful handbook for individuals at every level of the organisation, because we really are all leaders and influencers.

Lucy runs The Performance Business with her husband Michael McNulty and works as a consultant developing face to face communication excellence and Centred Leadership skills.

Many years ago, in the mid 1990's, when Lucy worked as a Sales Account Manager for Computacenter, one of her clients, Jane, once said to her "When I ask for cake Lucy, I just want cake. I don't want the cherry on the top."

It took Lucy years of research and learning to understand what she had meant (if you read the story about the baby and the stairs, you will untangle the mystery for yourself).

That one short conversation with Jane launched a commitment to really find out why some people seem to communicate effortlessly whilst others, equally passionate, caring and conscientious seem to miss the mark and rub people up the wrong way. This book is the culmination of that work.

When not writing or running the business, Lucy is a keen rower, a member of Molesey Boat Club. She is spouse of Mike, mother to Lydia, Max and walker and chief ball thrower for Dumbledore the dog.

Find out more about Lucy's work at

www.theperformance.biz

People Aren't Widgets

Lightning Source UK Ltd.
Milton Keynes UK
UKOW07f0607041114

241045UK00001B/61/P